Inspired by
My Museum

sampad is a registered charity no. 1088995

Inspired by My Museum

Edited by
Anne Cockitt, sampad
and
Rosalind Fursland,
University of Birmingham Cultural Intern at sampad

Published by
sampad and British Council

Published by sampad, South Asian Arts and British Council
c/o mac birmingham, Cannon Hill Park, Birmingham, B12 9QH UK

First Edition 2014

This selection and edition ©sampad 2014 and British Council, India

ISBN 978-0-9565416-4-2

Cover design by Mugdha Sadhwani
Cover photograph (c) Mat Wright, courtesy British Council

Printed by Arunima Printing Works
81, Simla Street, Kolkata 700006, WB, India
apw@vsnl.net

www.sampad.org.uk
www.britishcouncil.org.in/arts

Foreword

When I got my first job in a museum as a young man, in the 1980s, in Germany, my friends all thought I was mad. Back then, a museum meant dusty corridors, dreary exhibits, Sunday afternoons of stupefying boredom. Most people thought of visiting a museum as a penance, not a pleasure.

But museums were changing. The 1980s were a time of revolution in museum practice. The ideas that took hold then remain powerful: museums must fulfil a social purpose; the needs and interests of visitors are at the heart of their mission. Today, we see the results of this revolution. There are more museums and more museum visitors in the world than ever before.

This book is written by some of those many visitors. It records moments of inspiration that they have experienced in museums, large and small, across the world. When Sampad South Asian Arts and the British Council launched the 'Inspired By My Museum' competition in 2013 they received nearly 480 entries from 32 countries, from Canada to New Zealand.

The writers published in this book come from diverse communities and express diverse perspectives. One writer from Kolkata, India, describes how a few hours spent in the museum gave them a window on the entire world. Readers of this book may experience a similar sensation. I hope that you will enjoy this record of inspiration and that it will, in its turn, inspire and encourage you to walk through the doors of many more museums, in search of the world inside.

Martin Roth
Director, Victoria and Albert Museum

sampad is a dynamic south Asian arts organisation based in Birmingham, playing a significant role regionally and nationally in promoting the appreciation and practice of the arts originating from India, Pakistan, Bangladesh and Sri Lanka. The word sampad means wealth in Sanskrit and organisation translates this as cultural wealth to be shared as widely as possible.

The **British Council** creates international opportunities for the people of the UK and other countries and builds trust between them worldwide. We are a Royal Charter charity, established as the UK's international organisation for educational opportunities and cultural relations. Our 7000 staff in over 100 countries work with thousands of professionals and policy makers and millions of young people every year through English, arts, education and society programmes.

Introduction

'Museums inspire' ... yes they do and we have over 480 creative writers who responded to the call for this writing competition convincing us about that through their moving and emotive words. Reading them made me recall my own experience of many hours spent in the library of the Indian Museum in Kolkata, preparing for my Masters in Ancient History.

The response from 32 countries across the globe also highlights the phenomenal diversity of museums inspiring some very personal and emotional reactions from the writers. The depth, imagination and range of these works are staggering and impressive.

We are delighted to have partnered with the British Council, India and the Museums Association UK in realising this project. To all the writers who participated and the team of esteemed judges I extend a sincere and warm 'thank you'.

I hope this publication will make your next visit to the museum more interesting and inspiring!

Piali Ray OBE
Director, Sampad South Asian Arts

The 3 overall winning entries are:

India

Jaya Jain, *The Fall: Museum of Broken Relationships,*
Zagreb, Croatia

UK

Frances Gapper, *The Terror of the Oceans:*
Natural History Museum, London

Russia

Katherine Turkina, *Blank Verse of Shadow Theatre.*
K. Malevich. "Black Square": The State Tretyakov
Gallery, Moscow

Outstanding entries:

India

Ashwini Gowariker, *The Anchor of Wood:*
Auschwitz-Birkenau Memorial and Museum, Poland

Sharmila Mitra, *The Halls of Shadows: The Indian Museum,*
Kolkata

Gaurav Sharma, *Ugly/Beauty: The Louvre, Paris, France*

UK

Andrew Lemming, *Love Among the Exhibits: Various*

Lizzy Ridout, *Hanging Out: National Portrait Gallery,*
London

Kenneth Adams, *Inspired By My Museum: Fleetwood*
Museum, Lancashire

Highly Commended entries:

Canada
Jennifer Footman, *Astarte's Pendant: The Cyprus Exhibition, National Museum of Scotland, Edinburgh*

India
Adrija Bandyopadhyay, *Nikita's Arrival: The Indian Museum, Kolkata*
Shambhobi Ghosh, *In Time: The British Museum, London*
Mrudula Patil: *Museum of National History, New York*
Sharon Puthur, *The Handkerchief: The Prince of Wales Museum, Mumbai*
Neelam Saxena Chandra, *Mahatma: Anand Bhawan, Allahabad*

UK
Skye Bayley, *Trapped: Potteries Museum and Art Gallery, Stoke on Trent*

Andrew Campbell-Kearsey, *The Brighton Museum Cat: Brighton Museum, East Sussex*

Oran Crawford, *The Day I Met Evil: Auschwitz-Birkenau Museum, Poland*

Philip Howard, *Pauline in the Yellow Dress, Sir James Gunn, 1944: Harris Museum and Art Gallery, Preston, Lancashire*

Contents

USA

CANADA
Cheryl Braganza
Montreal, Quebec

My 1964 Sexual Awakening: Grosvenor Gallery, London, UK

Buttery daffodils swayed in the April breeze as I stepped out of the convent hostel in Kensington headed for Grosvenor Gallery in Mayfair. London, 1964. I was 19 years old, recently arrived from India, never having attended a gallery opening in my life. The exhibit entitled "The Human and Divine Predicament", the artist Francis Newton Souza, a Goan, like myself. The people there would be twice my age. I was nervous. Artists were to me, god-like.

Entering the gallery at 30 Davies Street, I squeezed through the crowd. As I stared at the wall of paintings, my eyes widened. Irreverent nudes with parted legs sprouting vulvas were splashed on magazine scraps. Beside them, delicate line drawings of Indian women broke through in contrast. Suddenly, intermittent pear-shaped faces, grotesque monster-like heads sketched almost haphazardly in ink appeared near bulbous breasts and genitalia. The distorted torso of a saint filled another frame. Images of Christ snorting fire from his nostrils and hanging stark naked from a cross had me perplexed. Was I in a den of sin?

"So what do you think, lady?" I spun around to the pock-marked bearded face of Souza, standing in an open shirt, blue jeans, corduroy jacket. "It's, er, nice." He roared with laughter, his breath charged with wine. "There's no need to say anything but as a fellow-Goan, let me explain. I paint to protest. See the eyes in the brow? This man sees with his brain. I use lines, arrows, stars, fish, rods savagely – everything is symbolic. Remember this, dear young

1

nymph - Art is a primeval force within human beings, in you and me. It keeps us alive. Understand? Now go drink and ogle." His eyes sparkled. Licking his lips, he slapped me on the back and disappeared into the noisy, adulating crowd.

I continued my slow trek through the gallery searching for meaning in his scribbles and scratches before I quietly left.

That brief interlude in the sixties with Indian art-icon Souza lit up something deep within. I learned to no longer relegate artists to higher realms and it gave me the impetus to become a committed painter myself. I mourned Souza's death in Goa in 2002.

For the past 50 years, painting has energised me and recently helped heal in my battle with cancer. Today I'm an art activist in Montreal focused on promoting human rights.

Jennifer Footman
Caledon, Ontario

Astarte's Pendant: The Cyprus Exhibition, National Museum of Scotland, Edinburgh, UK

I am made to stare at Astarte's Pendant
on display in this northern museum.
Circled by a bright spot light
in the dull, drear room
it's out of place: a diamond in a coal scuttle.

A small card assures viewers
there was indeed life east of Cyprus
once upon a time, a long time ago
when Scotland was little more than a bog
full of hairy men and low-slung women.

I fancy Astarte herself standing here,
she, who was forced to give up her near eastern practices
to become western, turn into that bitch
server of men: Aphrodite.

There must have been a cruel operation
in this alteration, a surgery with no pain killer.
Perhaps there was a sudden conversion, much
like the evolution of men
into slaves, or the one that changed
humans into slave owners,
so Astarte became Aphrodite.
Come on... Aphrodite has no sex
but exudes the fragrance of roses
and ancient deodorants demanded

to veil her shame of being a woman.
I love Astarte with all her stinks and imperfections,
she, who was proud of her good clean reek:
kippers and sweat and dried blood.

Nayoung Jin
Vancouver, British Columbia

Seahorse: The Beaty Biodiversity Museum Vancouver

A seahorse tail, holding gently
onto the finger of her care-taker,
who anxiously speaks
about overfishing of shrimp,
the staple diet for seahorses.

Mom,
do you remember?
I was two
when I gripped your finger with my right hand
to say how much I care about you.
Now, a grown-up, I
still wish to hold your finger
(with my invisible tail.)

A seahorse camouflages itself
when a predator looms closer.

In a faraway land,
whenever I encounter someone
who means to hurt me,
I make a wish
to turn into buttercups
or white button mushrooms.

Mom,
I am almost forest
while walking in the grass to hide.

CROATIA
Iva Tkalec
Varazdin, Varazdinska Zupanija

Ordinary Love: Museum of Broken Relationships, Zagreb

Once upon a time, very very far away, lived a beautiful young princess and a handsome young prince. As in every good love story, they fell in love. However, this is not a good love story. Word good got lost somewhere in between. The true story is that very near, maybe just around the corner, maybe even next door, lives a woman. Maybe she is young, maybe old. Maybe she is beautiful, maybe only average. Maybe little above the average. Looks are not really important in the end. Man is also here. Maybe not next door, maybe he really lives far far away, but at least transportation is more developed than in "once upon a time" time. So, the point is, their love was possible. However, something came in between their love and it was gone forever. One of them, the "more hurt" one, decided to save a little bit of good memories forever. Or maybe decided to leave agony behind. Or even anger. And saved it up in a museum.

They call it the "Museum of Broken Relationships". All pieces without meaning that once meant the most to someone, all tears collected in one simple letter, all promises broken, just as the toys once given as a Valentine's presents. They all belong in a museum. Ordinary, simple, every man's museum with exhibits that will never fade. Cheap exhibits with the price so low no one would buy them. But the ugliest, the dirtiest, the most torn up ones have the highest value. Strolling through a collection of meaningless things, meaningful tears are trying to come out. Wondering why everything is so familiar, yet only maybe the names are different. Names, ages, nationalities, religions...Don't we all have a teddy bear, a love letter, a shirt that was left behind, a book with a special note, playing cards or a door key... All of them crying out for their minute of fame.

Love seen through the love that was lost, maybe the most beautiful one. Everyone has a story. A love story. Behind every smiling face there is a sad one as well. Be kind, please be kind next time, every single one of them silently cries. We are all human after all. All same. All broken a little bit. We all belong to a museum. With a story that lives in every one of us.

FRANCE
Louise Robinson-Brouze
Grigny, Paris

An Awakening: The Egyptian Museum of Antiquities, Cairo, Egypt

"This way. This way", shouted Ali the guide, cutting through the swarms of tired yet wide eyed and excited tourists. There was hardly time to glance at the ancient relics. He waved his flag aloft, a tatty yellow scrap clinging to a worn, smooth bamboo stick. The humid air was intoxicating-ly intertwined with the scent of sweat and 'old' - musty, dusty and yet very much alive.

Senses on overload, I craned to keep track of Ali, frantically waving his yellow standard to keep his charges in tow. I flicked a glance left then right trying to absorb each glass encased element. Occasionally I checked ahead for a flash of familiarity, markers from the group who alighted the bus what seemed like only moments ago - yet an hour had already passed.

Skimming the artifacts of an age gone by, carriages, golden thrones, worn carved sphinx, we finally came upon the key which unlocked my box. My body buzzed from head to toe, my solar plexus tight and tingling, my breath high in my chest. Another age, a sense of 'knowing', invisible hands reached out to a kindred spirit on another plane. Standing almost silently, both in awe and with a strangely familiar sense of respect, around the glass tomb of a well preserved mummy I suddenly disappeared into that world - the shouts of men in harsh yet melodic Arabic; the dense smoky hue of burning wood and incense. Heavy plinths being laboriously hand-raised using thick rope, primitive hammers tapping away feverishly; the grimy sweat smeared bodies of dark and dusky men shining orange in the flickering light of the burning torches in this dark stone cave...or was it? My inner eye followed the symmetrical lines, row upon row of large grey-black blocks, steadily up towards the heavens and I understood. A brief glint of sparkling stars peeped through the uppermost unfinished soon-to-be point of this great pyramid.

"Madam please!" A frantic tug on my shirt sleeve brought me rushing back into my body, landing with an unceremonious thud. "Come, come, we go now," hastened Ali "Quick, quick madam." He rushed away like the pied piper followed by a trail of bouncing heads, still spinning from side to side trying to fit in a last memory.

For me, another small piece of the eternal puzzle fell into place as I took an unexpected step closer to my soul.

INDIA
Vinita Agrawal
Mumbai, Maharashtra

Priest King: National Museum, Karachi, Pakistan

Bearded, Soapstone Mohenjodaro man
you speak to
me in a white, low fired steatite voice
in these cold halls of the Karachi museum.
I bake your contemplations in my earthenware heart
drape your trefoil pattern cloak over my life
quietly inherit the hurt trapped in the maiolica amulet on
your arm.
Were you a river god?
A Priest King?
What questions did you drill into the universe
that I am still searching for answers 4500 years later?
Your faience figure bears no seal, no emblem, no resolve;
has no mercy on me.
I search your deeply incised eyes
with the same black sulphide kohl gaze
as the women in your days
but see only the missing inlays.
Some things never change.
I wonder if the sunlight streaming here through the hall's
vents
Is the same that fed your wheat.
I wonder if the chisel of time splintered milliseconds from
hours
back then too, to make strangers bond for life
in a fleeting, marauding, explosion called love.

I wonder if your best friend was pain,
like all the rest of us here and
if that was why you had turned to stone.
Your eyes say nothing, your lips not a word
But something slips from your heart to mine -
a little rolling stone of existence, still gathering moss.
Brick niches, coolie barracks, terra cotta walls around me
fill up with opaque white tin glaze symbols.
I know you have answers...
If only I could read them.
I return from the museum with your head fillet wrapped
around my soul.
I return with the feeling as though I've lived before.

Francis Anthony
Bengaluru, Karnataka

How Tropical Kerala Unearthed my Buried Cultural Memories: Mattancherry Palace, Kochi, Kerala

Irriguous Kerala's pregnant humidity brooded all around me, infusing each step I took towards Mattancherry Palace with sloth and sullen expectation. By western standards, the palace—built originally by the Portuguese around 1555 and "gifted" to the Cochin Raja—was not much to look at from the outside. It was a squat, low-slung, building with white stucco walls and sloping, reddish-brown-tiled roofs. Matronly, sari-clad commissionaires collected the meagre entry fee and carelessly ushered us in.

Inside, however, I was ensorcelled by the rampant greens and resplendent oranges of the many-splendored murals. With flamboyant illustrations from the Ramayana, the room dazzled with the majesty of traditional Keralan Hindu temple art. The rich tapestry in tempera evoked in me a million latent memories, sights, and smells. Of my father, a Malayalee Hindu, who had long ago abandoned me when I was still a child. (I was the inconvenient, ill-begotten love child at the cross-roads of competing religious and racial confessions.) Of time-worn, autochthonous Kerala Ayurvedic oils: I could almost smell the heavy head notes of camphor, clove, kayyoni, and amla. Or maybe that was simply the Malayalee woman beside me – her wet hair gleaming and fragrant with the oils of the morning's bath. She was viewing—unselfconsciously—a transcendent rendition of the queen Kausalya giving birth to Rama—her first born—her only born, the Man-God who would come to be acknowledged by Hindus as Maryada Purushottama—the

Perfect Man. The queen's legs were spread wide apart, supported by her ladies-in-waiting on both sides. The artist appeared to have limned this primal process without the slightest trace of inhibition. Despite my best efforts, I flinched ever so slightly at the sight. It's hard to shake off a buttoned-up Catholic upbringing.

I barely knew my father—I could only recollect him through disjointed memory slots, as though viewed through a View-Master. But oddly, this room and its myriad depictions of Keralan Hindu traditions stirred in me feelings I didn't know I possessed. Did Madhavan Kutty used to pray to Rama? Should I?

And yet, all this tradition was housed in a building designed and built by uninvited Portuguese interlopers, one of whom seeded my maternal ancestors and bequeathed to her the sobrenome of Colaço. And this complexity is the India I have known and come to cherish – complex, cosmopolitan, multi-confessional, and "unstraightforward." Apparently, God was capable of entertaining more than one thought in his (or her) mind at once.

Adrija Bandyopadhyay
Kolkata, West Bengal

Nikita's Arrival: The Indian Museum, Kolkata

Dr. Nikita Kundu, stood waiting at the arrival gate of Dum Dum Airport, Kolkata, after approximately 12 years.

'Bapti!'

No sooner did Nikita turn towards the sound of the voice, than she was enveloped in an all-encompassing hug. Nikita smiled. When baba finally released her, ma frowned severely. 'Why didn't you braid your hair?', she asked, 'and why aren't you wearing something to cover your chest?', she demanded gesturing towards the front of Nikita's T-shirt. No welcome back. No I love you. Nikita swallowed down the hurt she felt, quickly masking it with a stoic resignation. Her mother had always been this criticising and had always gotten on her nerves owing to her orthodox views, closed mind set and ignorance.

For some unexplained reason, her mother had always been against Nikita's going abroad. After Nikita had chosen to join one of the US colleges which had offered her a fellowship, her mother had been cold, and rather passive-aggressive…..

When Nikita opened the door to her old room, she had been expecting to find it as a storage area or a Thakur ghor. What she hadn't expected was to see her room exactly the way she had left it 12 years ago right down to the burn mark on the bedside table and the plastic fairy wand taped on her bed's headboard. For a moment she could actually feel her heart stop, and she held her breath, afraid to break the magic that had frozen her room in time.

Like in a museum, everything was on display. She gently held the clock that her school best friend had given her, and looked at her various Britney Spears, NSync, Lord of the Rings and Narnia posters that had become a craze for her in school. Her favourite books still adorned her bookshelves and her personal cards, chits and essays still hung from the inside of the doors of her closet. Her clothes were still there, albeit slightly dusty and smelling strongly of naphthalene.

Just as the museum is a gallery of artefacts and mementos of the past, so was this room an arcade of her own past.

When ma entered the room at sunset, Nikita got up from her childhood bed and for a moment mother and daughter simply stared at each other. In the glow of the setting sun they hugged.

Anneshya Banerjee
Kolkata, West Bengal

Inspired by My Museum: Netaji Museum, Giddapahar, Kurseong

It is perhaps a very true saying that great ideals are often inspired by something equally great. Netaji Subhas Chandra Bose has always been one of my idols ever since I had heard about his heroic tales from my father who too was an ardent worshipper of the figure. I had always dreamt of fighting for a noble cause like him though there obviously isn't an imperative of removing the binding chains of British colonialism from India anymore. Perhaps fighting for the rights of women in our society is a cause equally noble. Diligently working towards building myself a platform where someday I would step on and perhaps bring about a desired change have been my focus. I had shunned all possibilities of shifting from my bedrock until a chance encounter with a few letters and photographs changed everything.

During my last visit to Darjeeling, I had made up my mind to pay a visit to the Netaji Museum near Kurseong. Before I set my foot on the beautiful wooden house which used to belong to Sarat Chandra Bose since 1922 and where Subhas Chandra was placed for 7 months under house arrest by the British. I had expected to only see preserved items that boasted about the icon's remarkable journey as a freedom fighter and leader but apart from all this, what left me bedazzled are the icon's love letters and his photographs with his wife Emily Schenkl and their daughter Anita Bose.

First of all, the very thought that Netaji, a man of such stature could even love a woman and that too with all due respect since their marriage in Vienna was done in a "hindu" fashion(as was mentioned in one of the letters by Emily to Sarat Bose), in itself a matter of great awe. Netaji's love life was kept under the wraps and pretty much from the public eye because of several reasons due to which I like many others wasn't aware. After the matter seeped in, I felt a surge of happiness and a rush of pride and respect for the great hero.

I sat down for a while and wondered why I had shunned love and the beauty it brings with itself. Works of great cause often needs the cushioning of happiness and delight that love provides. It opens our eyes to colourful painted canvas of the world. I left the place with a hope in my heart and a smile on my face.

Ishani Banerji
Kolkata, West Bengal

In Midst Of Oblivion: The Indian Museum, Kolkata

I held her hand as we
Walked the cemented path
Entering the House of Fossils.
"Do you remember this place?"
I asked, she only faced
Me with a muzzled countenance.
"Never mind Dear,"
I heard my voice say.

She supported me as
We climbed one step at a
Time, my agility had slackened
Due to arthritic limbs.
She glanced at the
Stuffed rare animals
As the smell of disinfectant
Tickled my olfactory apparatus.

We were walking past
Myriad specimens and skeletons
Before my wife halted
In front of a glass jar.
A six month old human foetus
Was swimming in formalin.
It had never opened its
Eyes to look at the world.
"I wish our baby was alive,"
My beautiful wife sighed.

I looked at her amazed!
"Life would have been different
Had I had the power to
Conceive again after giving
Birth to our stillborn,"
She added in a plaintive voice.

Her rolling tears made me
Jocund. Dementia could not
Always overpower my wife.
In midst of oblivion
Her memory flickered
And shone bright.
This Museum always held
An emotional spot for us.

Fifty years before we
Were betrothed,
The museum sealed
Our future together.
Again the museum
Managed to defeat
Dementia and brought
My wife to me.

Although I knew very well
This bliss was transient,
She trusted me yet.
The evil disease had
Rooted itself in her
Brain and made her
Forget her existence and
Others revolving around her.

"Do not be sad, you are
All that matters to me,"

I comforted her.
"Let us enjoy the moment
And go for lunch,"
I suggested. She clutched my
Hand as we strolled out
Of the museum.

Siddhartha Basak
Kolkata, West Bengal

Home: The British Museum, London, UK

Are children really from anywhere? We landed at five thirty in the evening. We click-clacked across the walk-alator, through the security, and through the tunnels which looked like they were made of shiny tin foil. Mum and Dad went over to the counter while we were left to baggage-sit. Standing behind an iron fence separating the bus terminal from the car park, I looked up at the English sky above. Mocking me. You will leave soon, it said. Like you always do. The ride around London was tedious. Mum wanted to see it. Indians, like all tourists, have a thing for capitals. How can you tell your friends you've been to England if you haven't even seen the precious things the English have taken from your country? British Museum it was.

Aimlessly, I wandered through the labyrinthine paths between the exhibits. Not everything was new to me. I had been here once before. I had begged my parents to see the Rosetta Stone. I remember a thought which had passed through my mind at the time, evanescent and childish. The thought that, having wanted to see it so bad, it would probably be the only thing from England I would remember in subsequent years. I hadn't been entirely right, but today, as I walked up to the object of my eternal fascination, the trilingual key which had unlocked the scripts of Egypt, the memory flared into brilliance once more. I was THIS close to it. I could feel the sensation on my nose and fingers, almost as if a gust of ancient wind was passing through the glass to remind me of things not quite so ancient. As if the Stone was calling me. It was reminding me of what it had seen in me all those years ago. That glow in the eyes that since then faded to grief, and longing for the country I had

21

been taught not to call home. The mother I had been taken from in my infancy. It was telling me to remember that it had not forgotten me. That I was just the child who had been fascinated by its enthralling tale so many years ago. That rocks in a Museum could hold more meaning than all human endeavours to crack the hieroglyphs. That it did not care where I was from. For are children really from any-where?

Divyesh Bhandari
Karnataka, Bangalore

Museum Man: Leeds City Museum, UK

This man had a face-
Yes, a face.
A face that mirrored the very fortunes
Of that which he bore.

A criss – cross of lines,
Running from nowhere to everywhere
With a pale and puckered nose sitting at its centre,
And to top it all
A Geometry of wild wrinkles.

He held in his voice vestiges of time,
All raucous and proper,
In his black suit,
Polished shoes and ironed tie,
Walking to and fro,
As though-
These statues of bronze,
These sculptures,
These coins ,
These ruining artifacts,
Were all his inheritance.

He was decaying,
Living on an extended retirement,
Sleeping under the dinosaur,
Eating with the barbarians,
His home was a home of ages,
And this age was the age of confluence,

Mixing and merging past and future.
Many came, many went,
Both people and monuments,
Some stayed,
Some stored,
In the hallway-
In the attic,
Or just dismantled.

He brought me a book-
With the excitement of a peevish schoolboy,
It said Shakespeare's First Folio,
There was pride on his trembling fingers,
As he opened the book with tweezers,
Coughing, yet with a pipe in his hands,
He let out the smoke
Circling from his mouth
Blurring his countenance.

The joy with which he explained
The life of Keats and that of Donne,
Testimonies of wars and alibis of nuns,
He had seen the Pope and met the Queen,
Lived the World Wars and heard Presley,
And trusted his memory
Of living with zeal.

Each foot that walked that cobblestone
Each hand that built that dome
Each woman that sold and was sold
Each hawker that shouted
Each painter that captured
Each poet that expressed
Each rich that constructed
Each jewel, medal, badge, crown and robe that remains
Each merciless officer
Each active revolutionist

Each scientist that invented
Each parish priest
And of course the historian!
It is there that he lives today
An embodiment of time,
Our archival man,
My Museum Man.

Megha Chatterjee
New Delhi

Kurusura Submarine Museum: Vishakhapatnam

On a vacation to Vishakhapatnam last summer, while strolling along the R.K. beach, I came across a magnificent submarine - the INS Kurusura that had once served the Indian Navy and protected our waters for 31 years before it was decommissioned and turned into a museum.

Every corner of the huge vehicle had been utilised; the only empty space being the isle that connected all the rooms. Inside the submarine, were dummies which displayed how the divers had lived. The bed rooms were tiny and it was hard to imagine how they must have squeezed themselves into their beds. I stepped close to one of the dummies and for some strange reason, felt that its face was grave and sad. The voice of the curator seemed to get distant; the people around me slowly began to disappear and my surrounding became blurred.

I found myself on the deck among sailors who were gearing up for some action. The deafening alarms quelled the sound of orders being shouted out by the officers even as a huge crash was heard on the starboard side. The enemy troop was gaining on us and they had completely destroyed the starboard side of the sub. Beads of sweat rolled down my forehead. "I couldn't die here. What about my friends, family and future?" While looking for cover, I saw a sailor hurriedly end his telephone conversation saying, "Daddy has to work Princess but he will be back soon and then we can play all day long. Take care of your mom till then." When he hung up, his cheeks were wet. He knew that it might be the last time that he was speaking to his daughter. Quietly, he walked away and proceeded to join his comrades.

His silhouette faded and my surrounding became clearer. I was relieved to realize that it had just been a vision!

That is when it realise on me that our soldiers give up their comfortable lives to protect our country while we fret about petty things. They don't even complain about not being able to spend time with their families. We are often lost in our own lives and fail to appreciate what others do to keep us safe. Realisation dawned and I vowed, "No more complaining about petty issues for me!"

Madhulika Dutta
New Delhi

Dreams: National Museum, New Delhi

Feeling that a visit to the museum would do us both good, give my mother a much needed vacation from her household work and make my 11-year old self somewhat more knowledgeable, we decided to make the trip to the National Museum. Basking under the glorious spring sun, the museum's impressive facade took me by surprise. I was expecting a dilapidated place. Guarding age-old secrets, housing evidence of our past-the bloody battles, mighty conquests, uprooted civilisations, the place had to look, ancient, I felt. I tugged at my mother's arm, urging her to hurry up and buy our tickets.Hand in hand we strolled through the various display cases showcasing pottery, seals, jewellery, terracotta figurines, tools and a human skeleton that scared me witless. All the cases had labels on them, bearing information about the objects on display. My mother read out and explained them to me.We had reached a case showing a metal figurine of a dancing girl. Mother said that women occupied a respectable position in society during the time of the Indus Valley civilisation, the figurine was proof of it. This wasn't written on the label. "How do you know that?" I asked her suspiciously. She smiled a sad smile and said, "I am an arts graduate. History was my major at college. I had a liking for the subject from the very beginning and was the only student from my college to have qualified for a Master's degree in the museology course. But I was 22 then and we weren't so well off to invest further in my education. My father had died years back and my mother's only anxiety was to see me well settled. So she had me married to your father." Her eyes had moistened.

"I had of thought of continuing my education after marriage but one cannot break free of the ties of domesticity so easily. Never compromise on your dreams, darling. They keep alive the spark in your eyes and the sense of achievement in your heart."I didn't make much of it then but know better now. A woman has as much right to live her dreams as a man and should not give up on them even if society expects it of her. I would have to be a fool not to learn from my mother's mistake and she has not raised me to be one, you see.

Manaswita Ghosh
Balasore, Odisha

An Imagination from the Past, an Inspiration for the Present: Victoria Memorial Hall, Kolkata

I am a writer. Not one of the famous ones who sign books or attend press conferences. I am rather the modest one, with a handful of works to my credit. Museums have always fascinated me, ever since I can recall. They make me remember history in their own, mysterious way.

But it was never a life-changing experience until I visited Victoria Memorial, Kolkata. It inspired me to heights I had never imagined. I do not credit any particular antique in the museum for this, but a restricted corridor in the back of the building, which I happened to spot accidentally. I was looking for the stairs that would take me to the ground floor, and there it was; the restricted corridor.

I was awestruck by the view – A lone corridor that gave in to a grand window, which faced the lawn. It was about four in the evening, and I could see sunlight dance on the marble floor of the corridor. A grandfather clock stood in a corner, but I couldn't see the time, as it wasn't facing me. A settee occupied the space in front of the grandfather clock, its creamy leather seat inviting me to cross the restricted line. I couldn't help but be amazed at the view that was in front of me; and I wondered if anyone had ever stood here as I did today and had taken the time to marvel at the sunlight casting its reminisces on the floor. Something as simple as a grandfather clock and a settee allowed the mind to rush to times it had never witnessed. I wondered if it had been made in England. If a young lady had ever sat on it with her gown flowing on the floor; her chin in her hands;

her locks all the way down her waist, bouncing in the sunlight; and thought about the man she was engaged to be married to. Did she look out of a window similar to the one that stood before me? Did she feel the ancient breeze on her face, the sunlight embracing her? I was lost.

And right then, I realised a hundred things. My life was just a granule in the vast ocean of time. I had to be someone significant before I was lost. So, someday, years from now when I am gone, a girl my age looks at my books and imagines – Me.

Shambhobi Ghosh
Kolkata, West Bengal

In Time: The British Museum, London, UK

Walking through these doors,
you would tell yourself
that you have seen the entire world
within two ephemeral hours.

Or parts of the world
that really matter, anyway;
the rich parts, the splendid, mysterious pasts,

all that came in time
out of a million human thoughts -
now embalmed in a single treasure room.

And as you walk past
the rows of porcelain,
the bronze figurines,
the strange looking things in between
you are quite unsure of,
and rocks as old as the universe,
the enormity of it all makes you forget
of all that it is worth.

But it does occur to you
every now and then
that nothing, or almost nothing
really ever belonged here in the first place,
to them, to you, or to anything at all
outside.

The next door leads you to
the room of the dead -
memories of those human thoughts
embalmed along your last footfall
in your room of pasts.

Ashwini Gowariker
Pune, Maharashtra

The Anchor of Wood: Auschwitz-Birkenau Memorial and Museum, Poland

When your parents had asked you to choose one thing to take on the journey, you had picked the ruler.

In your nine-year old universe of hand-me-down clothes, boots and school-books, the ruler had been one of the first new things you had owned. Its unbroken edge had caught the glow of the lamp, swishing exciting promises when your brother had swung it like a sword. The other boys at school had been envious, and you had felt benevolent letting them hold the treasure.

But these weren't your reasons for wanting to take the ruler with you.

It was the row of numbers that entranced you. Etched into the burnished wood of the ruler, the numbers were matte black, and unmoved by the vagaries of light and the moods of your teachers.

They didn't waver and distort, like the vows your friend and you had once scratched into a tree trunk.

Like the men in uniform who had marched into your house to bark out questions, striding out before your father had answered them.

Like your mother's promise to comfort you every time you had nightmares.

The sign which assured you that work would set you free.

The wave of sleep that overwhelmed you every day while you were sieving cement, and which miraculously evaporated as you lay in your bunker at night. Or the racking cough of the boy bundled next to you, who had disappeared just when you had learnt to find comfort in the sound.

Perhaps you had thought of the numbers on your ruler when they herded you into the crowded room that morning. But if by then, you had too much on your mind to remember the past, I want you to know that you were right.

The numbers didn't let you down. They are as uncompromising and constant as you had believed them to be. Left to the mercies of a world of shifting beliefs and actions, the ruler is duller, and its edge is not as immaculate as it had once been.

But even sixty nine years later, the numbers on the ruler have not yielded. I've seen them myself, holding their own against the refraction of the glass case and the harsh fluorescent lights in exhibit 11, at the Auschwitz-Birkenau Memorial and Museum.

Anjali Gupta
Kolkata, West Bengal

Impressions...: Albert Hall Museum, Jaipur, Rajasthan, India

Today was just like any other day. The caretaker was present with the blower in his hands. I was standing against the wall. I smiled, putting up a pretty face but he didn't smile back. Hmph! Rude.

He took me and spread me out against the wall, murmuring simultaneously, "Damn! This carpet needs hell of a maintenance." And I retorted back, "Well, I am not some show-piece in any ordinary shop. Good Luck finding a golden carpet. And yes, I'm high maintenance. Deal with it!!" And he got about his work without muttering a word, ignoring whatever I said. Ha! Gotcha.

While he was blowing the dust away from my beautiful golden zari and Persian silk border, I looked around. The golden tiffin box smiled and the jade and silver figurine waved. I smiled back. But something else seemed to be bothering me. Like a feeling that today might not be like the other days. And the coming days might never be like today.

The afternoon sun shone brightly through the French windows; buttercup rays filling up the otherwise dark room. I and my friends aren't for public display. So we're kept in a room, hidden and secured.

The caretaker finished his job and shifted his attention to Mrs.Teacup. The door was ajar and I was looking at the people passing by; unaware of my presence.

And then it happened.

Where people were rushing, she suddenly stopped. And turned to face me. This had never happened before. Hadn't she got someplace else to go? To some other room? And hard as I tried to ignore her, her piercing eyes brought my attention back to her. And I saw it.

Her eyes grew bigger in awe; her pupils dilating. Even my old enemy-turned-friend, Time, froze. She looked at me from top to bottom; her gaze never flickering even for a split second.

And for the first time in many years I felt that forgotten feeling again – being seen as something special.

"She would forever remember this day; Me. She might not remember this museum and I might become a vague memory but now at this moment I know I won't be forgotten. Anyhow. Ever."

"I will forever remember this day; that carpet. The Golden Carpet. Where many don't even know about its existence, I saw it. I may not remember this museum but this....this will never be forgotten."

Nita Idnani
Ahmedabad, Gujarat

A National Museum on The Life and Works of Sardar Patel: Sardar Memorial-Ahmedabad

My tuition kids were all jumpy and excited when I told them that we would be visiting Sardar Patel National Memorial. The Sardar Patel Museum is housed in the Moti Shahi Mahal in the Shahibaug area. Surrounding the Moti Mahal is an open garden dotted by peacocks and monkeys. When we got there, I paid for the entrance tickets and we walked into the museum. A small statue of Sardar rests at the entrance of the museum. His memorial is spread across the ground floor, covering the central hall and four adjacent rooms. The museum traces his life through pictures, portraits, biographical descriptions, political cartoons, clippings from newspapers, relics and personal possessions. I tried to explain some of the scenes which were portrayed to help both the children to understand the past. Soon the kids got interested and started asking questions. I am sure they learnt more that day by looking at the modelled displays than they could ever have by just reading lessons in the textbooks. Along with the museum, the memorial also houses two multi media halls. We were invited to watch a documentary film, but the children were too restless to sit down and watch a historical movie and so I declined. In the basement we found a long endless corridor which displays innumerable, colourful paintings of the 1857 freedom struggle heroes along with some glimpses of the Andaman Cellular Jail. Manini who is keen to take up painting as a full time career looked at the portraits with a lot of interest. Information of 562 erstwhile princely states, their flags and coins are on display on the first floor. One room has been dedicated to Rabindranath Tagore who spent six months at this place. It carries his memory through portraits, pictures and a statue of this great son of India. Aditya liked the statue of a British soldier in red uniform and even saluted him. He said he would grow up and become a soldier so that he could wear such nice clothes. The three of us thoroughly enjoyed ourselves that day at the museum. I realised how valuable such museums were as they taught us many things.

Deepa Kylasam Iyer
Puducherry

Wall Paper: La Tour de la Lanterne, La Rochelle, France

You sit waiting for the wild water locks
To part, new passages to open to other
Promised lands, through a tiny window
That frames your feverish demands
Of life. The sly rust on your chains
Inks poetry on the yellowing wall.
Hope is a wallpaper full of indecipherable
Graffiti, your heart's murmurs, its innocuous call

To salt, wine and cheese, away from
This foul prison drenched in the blood
Of Catholic priests. To a woman perhaps,
And to the warmth of love, perfectly poised
To shoot out a fountain of children.
A piece of land, savage soil
That you tempt and tease to
Produce, toil that yields legends,
Unearths scandals and reaps bloodless
Grandchildren.

You sulk with long summer evenings
Watching love's curious mutations,
And give over to silent gratification
Of unblocking the clog and repairing the drains
Of a vehemently tender nuptial strain,
And become the ugly, useful animal-
A wife's faithful dog.

Or spend that bitter winter brooding
In the careful alcove of your petty vices,
Your joyless search concluding
In unreturned caresses, your
Spineless nightmares collapse
Into bottomless abysses
Of pain and guilt and shame.

You head carefully towards the mundane
Chocked with your devices, numbed by
Unwelcome surprises. By now,
The house you lovingly built
For your wife and children
Is a desolate graveyard of silence,
Yearning a new way of life
And a wallpaper.

So, you write again on the yellowing
Pages of a yellowing world;
How terror wrestled agonies,
Or fear presided over prayers
At the Lantern Tower.
How desires sprung astonishingly
From a life defiled. How the search for redemption
Ended in the vestiges of life and an
Inventory of 'what to do'
Dissolved into unkempt rendezvous

With life. Now, you are a carte blanche
Your face a cheque annulled
Of private desires. Prying eyes
Fossilise your prayers, the cold
Hands of Time has stuffed
Your poetry into the gangrene of modern
Curiosity. History, as you lived it,
Every slow minute of your life

Arrested by your steady heartbeats
Is silenced. Each passing year
In this museum takes away
The last few breaths of your
Heart, hope and death.

Jaya Jain
Vadodara, Gujarat

The Fall: Museum of Broken Relationships, Zagreb, Croatia

Fell?
I guess he knew that well.

You go deep... deeper into him.
It's like gravity working you in.
Slowly, beautifully...
It's mesmerizing
So overwhelming and tantalizing.

Take a deep breath,
Close your eyes
And take the fall.
Plunge into the unknown
You give in to it.
And that is what probably was your fault.

Do not open your eyes,
It's a warning.
Feel it.
It is something better just felt.
It's a subtle beginning...
Soft, warm.
And then it hits you.
A passion, a burning desire.
So strong that it makes you wanna look,
Look at what is it that you are craving.
Hear if there is something that he is saying.
You don't want to just feel it anymore.
You want to scream
And announce to the world that he is yours.

And then there is a pause.
A sudden stop in the fall.
Like he is letting go…
You are slipping away…
You want to grab something and hold on.
But all you find is thin air.

Hysterical. Scared. Frightened.
You open your eyes.
Stupid girl.

You realise you are succumbed.
The gravity acted at its worst.
This is a black hole.
It's all darkness.
You hear a silence so loud that it makes you deaf.
There is no way out.
It is suffocating.
You are choked.

Cold. Brutal. Tragic.
Pain that makes you numb.

Betrayal. Abandonment. Emptiness.
For you this is the end.

His desire, fulfilled.
His want, satisfied.
You, used.

Fell?
He definitely knew that well.
You wanted to LIVE?
Well, he spelled it backwards
And shoved it in your face.
And you definitely did not know THAT well.

Mukul Kumar
New Delhi

The Remnants of Independence: Swatantrata Sangram Sanghralaya, Red Fort, Delhi

"For years, we have been lying here, enclosed in this show-case, to display the story and the events that took place on this land. We have gulped a history in us and a plethora of emotions. It suffocates in our studded sheaths. As we were meant to be held in hands and to be stabbed into the enemy's body. We have witnessed the wars our master had fought on this battlefield, on this motherland. All those purple patches on us, the blood of thousands slain, we have soaked.

But we do regret, as we lay here in guilt,we could not be useful to our master to save his life and his valiant body. We gaze at the people in despair, in wait of a powerful soul who has vigour in his blood, who will hold us back to relieve the suffering of the people. But we are proud that we belonged to such a man, who sacrificed his life to save the integrity of this motherland. We are full of pride to say that we are the swords of Nana Rao Peshwa, a freedom fighter who led a series of revolts and uprisings to fight against agrarian breakdown that resulted from a feudal state.

We feel sad that we could not make the people free, but we feel good to look at the stick in the statue of man standing in front of us, who freed India. Though we are full of rage and are the weapons of malice, we are greatly inspired by that. Even by being a stick, it is not just a stick of violence but of reverence and fortune which led many people and headed them. To march forward and achieve the greatest joy of millennium of independence-What a great achievement!.......

And next to us, is a letter of protest renouncing knighthood, written by Rabindranath Tagore, it reveals the accounts of suffering undergone by the people and the universal agony of indignation roused in the hearts of Indians that had been ignored by the rulers. All wonder, but only a few can understand what value these badges, shields, dioramas, sculptures, lithographs, guns and pistols have.

Today also when we remember those days of freedom struggle, we are filled with nationalism which goes beyond the limits of this Swatantrata Sangram Sanghralaya and beyond the boundaries of Red Fort!!....."

Sreya Mallika Datta
Kolkata, West Bengal

Inconsequentiality: Museo Nacional Del Prado, Madrid, Spain

Look. There they are. In time-trapped frames of
Eternity.
There, just beyond the pillar, Saturn
Devours his peach-fleshed son.
His frenzied eyes dissolve into
Death
plucking out life, for a moment more of existence.
And there, sportive cherubs flirt-flit around the Poet;
The crown of Inspiration is a laurel-second away from his
head.
Only if you look, you might chance upon
Colossus and catch yourself in a stifled gasp
That dies in your throat, unborn.
The night merges into his waist as
he rises above the whispering hills
where men are strewn like rage-torn strips of
Childhood paintings.
A sun
ny grace-day.
A dog curled up on its paws is
about to yawn at Jesus washing his disciples' feet.
Have you ever felt the twilight-waters
of a river once kissed by the sun?
Down the hallway,
An artist paints the infant Margarita.
Margarita, who is forever caught on the
Blossoming
Bud of womanhood.

He will paint till the edge of time,
For he himself is painted,
Always a brush-stroke short of the final touch.
When you cannot walk any more,
You may just come across Sisyphus.
The jagged weight of his rock
reminds us of the times when we have lost our
Dreams
Only to remember they were never ours to lose.
Yet, we must go on. Must
we?
And just for a razor-edge moment, we
wait for time to stop.
A spider's web moment.
Tick, tick, tick.
History breaks out of its frame and
Spills into the world where you are.
All time is here, now, All at once.
Fade. And look upon yourself—
Lost, amidst the mist-maze of Time;
Trapped in a little burst-bubble of
Inconsequentiality.

(Note: the paintings referred to in this poem, in order of allusion are: Saturn
devouring his son- Rubens, Peter Paul; Parnassus-Poussin, Nicholas; The
Colossus- Follower of Goya; The Foot Washing-Tintoretto, Jacopo Robusti;
Las Meninas, or The Family of Felipe IV-Velázquez, Diego Rodríguez de Silva y,
where Velázquez portrays himself, painting the painting itself, on the left of the
canvas; and Sisyphus- Titian)

Sharmila Mitra
Kolkata, West Bengal

The Halls of Shadows: The Indian Museum, Kolkata

A sudden shout from the Form Teacher;
"Silence! Girls, we're going to the museum
Next Thursday, starting at ten, sharp. Bring
Your own water bottles, no food from home, nothing but
water. All clear?"

That was a lot of years ago, when I was but
Nine or ten. Since then
I have been inside this museum but once more.
But I can conjure up the halls and the endless corridors,
And the arches, the pillars, the glass top cabinets, the
Motes of dust dancing in a beam of sunlight.

Museum... a night in the museum would've been nice,
I've always thought, often caught
Myself letting loose a flight of fancy,
A chance to see mummy return to life,
Or a fossil soften, melt, become a whole new life.

A museum is a place full of shadows
Of times and things and people past
In the rush of liquid time, like a prime
River, like the Euphrates, the Tigris, the Nile...
A museum is a place of frozen time,
A home for things past their prime;
But, it's not a place like a cemetery
Full of tombstones, or occasional living groans.

A museum is a place of shadows,
Golden, ashen, greyish, brownish,
Greenish, reds, whites, yellows,
All muted and quiet, like footfalls
Of someone stalking you as you view
Ancient remnants of the unseen past
Archived in the hollow spaces of the museum.

When I think of the museum,
I am filled with shadows of tears
That fall freely but do not wet the face,
Leave no trace,
But soften the rough edges of my daily drudgery,
And raise an earthy scent from the dust,
As if the smell of the rain on the Earth's crust.

Archita Mittra
Kolkata, West Bengal

The Silent Storyteller: Kolkata Panorama (Town Hall), Kolkata

History lies imprisoned in a glass cage,
Fallen warriors frozen in place,
Their coats gleaming, their eyes still,
Their swords ready to kill.

The grey shadows on white-washed walls,
Can they not hear the clarion call?
Do they not hear the blood-curdling screams,
Echoing in their fading dreams?

This museum chronicles the struggle for independence,
Of a land sinking in the snares of decadence,
A history forged of plastic and clay,
The history of our darker days.

I breathe the sordid tales, the suppressed femininity
Smell the room freshener, the veiled modernity
They preserve that which will decay,
The hours won't linger; I cannot stay.

I can hear the lazy shuffle of feet,
The past has nothing left to teach,
The past has washed over me like a wave,
This is but a slow walk to the grave.

I am a fool, to preserve the illusory,
The decaying remnants of youthful beauty,

But I wasn't made for your feast,
I am not your museum showpiece.

Freedom is a birth right,
You can say it with delight.
You can convince the children, but you can't convince
me.
For the woman is never truly free.

Make a martyr from our tales,
Make music from our dying wails,
Save our rags for the last,
Preserve the dresses behind the glass.

The museum is a silent storyteller
It tells the children of our past,
I am a silent storyteller
I tell stories with my scars.

Arpita Mittra
Kolkata, West Bengal

The Museum of Museums: The Heritage of North Kolkata

Oh! Kolkata! How wonderful you are! So old, fragile yet full of rich heritage. Once a city of palaces and British colonial rule is now a city of newly built flyovers and houses of varied geometric designs. You resemble a museum on a grand scale

Walking through the alleys of north Kolkata, you find such marvellous buildings of great architectural beauty. Some are as old as the city itself-huge, spacious and full of antiques. To name a few-Marble Palace, Jorasanko Thakur Bari, Sovabazar Rajbari, Mittra Bari and various others. They were owned by men of rich culture and refined tastes. Entering these houses you find unique antiques and object-de-art well preserved.

One such house-owner is himself a better curator than that of any other public museum. A visit to his home was a life-transforming experience. His knowledge of history, geography, literature, science and metaphysics was overwhelming. Like the old buildings resting on Doric columns with spacious rooms and verandahs with high ceilings, this man exuded his vast knowledge of the world.

This man also guided me through the secrets of Kolkata and we visited Victoria Memorial, National Library, Metcalfe-Hall, High Court, Legislative Assembly and the entire BBD Bag Area. The city with its varied culture ranging from European, Chinese, Jewish, Muslim, Parsi, Jain, Bengali is brimming with life.

The markets of Kolkata takes one down the memory lane where you get a gamut of all the ingredients required for a culinary feast. Food items of all nations combine and mingle together to form a communal fountain. Religions of various hues are celebrated with great fervour and the city throbs with old wisdom blended with youthful vigour. At the end of the day, sitting on a wrought iron seat in the Maidan, watching the sun set and the golden horizon transforming into deep darkness, the city traversed and guided by this man came to a total stand still. The birds have stopped chirping. All the citizens weary, after a hard day's toil have trodden their way home, leaving me behind gaping at the sky.

This man at his ripened old age is himself a museum. When he started unfolding like the petals of a flower, the fragrance is still lingering on in my mind.

Alas! A museum can be restored but a man's life can never be regained. It can only be embalmed with love, respect and remembrance. With gratitude I pay a visit to his home which reminds me of enriching experiences.

Utsa Mukherjee
Kolkata, West Bengal

Me and my Colours!: National Museum of Bhutan, Paro, Bhutan

 I walked into the crowded hall.
Paintings hanging on its walls.
And people training their eyes upon them.

The smells chocked my nostrils
-flowers, paintings, articles and dust.
Statues freezing time to a standstill,
Time freezing itself amongst the people.

Suddenly, everybody pressed to the corners
and vanished.
- melting minds, melting people.
Time froze to a standstill.

All those colourful people,
frozen here for centuries
- stuck on the wall, hammered to the ground,
started pouring their Self upon me!

A light blasted in my conscience.
I opened my eyes.
I saw my Other, painted in multi-coloured hues,
right before my discoloured Self.

The colours upon my grey matter,
The colours upon my eyes.
Me, mine and my colours,
and your colours, O paintings, are upon mine!

Juhi Neogi
Kolkata, West Bengal

My Visit to the Bard's Home: Tagore Museum, Jorasanko Thakur Bari, Kolkata

A certain field trip in November
Change my perspective towards art
In my very city did I visit
A palace very close to my heart,

Home to my country's most prolific writer
Winner of world recognition and fame,
There is more to him and his home
Than the eyes does see and words do name...

It is a mansion built by a 'prince'
Not fallen into the ruins of time,
Not washed away like footprints in sand
Stands erect that palace sublime -

It encloses something more,
Something more to awe-inspire,
A museum as is it called
With more than exhibits to admire.

In all modesty, I do confess
I was not in an artistic bent of mind,
When I gazed at the poet's paintings
The museum was one of its kind.

From that day hence,
I visited many a museum, galleries of art,
But the noble home of Jorasanko
Etched a mark in my heart.

Mrudula Patil
Navi Mumbai, Maharashtra

Museum of National History, New York, USA

You'll find labels describing what is gone:
an empress's bones, a stolen painting

of a man in a feathered helmet
holding a flag-draped spear.

A vellum gospel, hidden somewhere long ago
forgotten, would have sat on that pedestal;

this glass cabinet could have kept the first
salts carried back from the Levant.

To help us comprehend the magnitude
of absence, huge rooms

lie empty of their wonders—the Colossus,
Babylon's Hanging Gardens and

in this gallery, empty shelves enough to hold
all the scrolls of Alexandria.

My love, I've petitioned the curator
who has acquired an empty chest

representing all the poems you will
now never write. It will be kept with others

in the poet's gallery. Next door,
a vacant room echoes with the spill

of jewels buried by a pirate who died
before disclosing their whereabouts.

I hope you don't mind, but I have kept
a few of your pieces

for my private collection. I think
you know the ones I mean.

Sharon Puthur
Bangalore, Karnataka

The Handkerchief: The Prince of Wales Museum, Mumbai

'Isn't it a wonder what you find in a museum?'

The speaker was a girl I had been admiring since our wait in the queue to enter The Prince of Wales museum or now The Chhatrapati Shivaji Maharaj Vastu Sangrahalaya.

'You see those items? Those are the most intimate belongings of a human. An earthen pot, a wooden doll, a necklace of shells; these were used by somebody, regular basic things, maybe cherished, maybe not, but valued and prided over by people now. Don't you think it strange?' I nodded happily. We walked together discussing at length, pausing respectfully to appreciate the beauty of an artefact or two.

At closing time I asked her out to coffee but she refused.

'I have a flight to catch to Bangalore. It is my last day in Mumbai and where better to spend it than here? I marry next week.'

When she left with the taxi I was filled with a strange incompleteness.

A piece of fabric on the ground caught my attention. The handkerchief was a simple square of cotton adorned with a pink embroidered 'A'. A regular item, maybe cherished, maybe not.

I smiled as I glanced at the museum behind.

I would treasure it.

Mythili Rao
Bangalore, Karnataka

The Threshold: Museum at Jaipur and Delhi

Stepping over the threshold
A silence
Welcoming me into its folds,
Murmuring whispers from the distant past.
Stories of victories and defeats
of bravery and deceits,
of desire and greed,
business and trade,
temples and faith,
of egos lying in dust,
of life and death
Nurtured by the rivers,
The earth, the sun
And taken by them too!
Pots and pans,
Wars of clans,
Treasures from the folds of earth.
Pictures of grandeur
Carved on stone,
Singing the songs
Of the yesteryears.
The swords so sharp,
The diamond so bright,
Bringing out the truth
From darkness to light.
Echoes of the distant past
Breathing fire then
Dust and ashes today
Weaving a story

Of life gone away, far
into the deep recesses
of consciousness.
Beckoning "come to me".
"You are no better than what you were"
Whither do they go?
Questions galore.
Civilisations-
the making of mankind.
The sands of time,
Blowing away the footprints
Grappling at the straw
Lest it drown you away.
Taking you to the land of the living dead.
Or is it the dead who live forever!

Neelam Saxena Chandra
Lucknow, Uttar Pradesh

Mahatma: Anand Bhawan, Allahabad

As I watched the room
Which Mahatma Gandhi
Used to inhabit
When he visited Anand Bhawan,
My eyes were full of pride
And my hands went up involuntarily
To salute
The great visionary.

How modest was he,
Despite having so much
Name and fame!

Awed I was of the fact
That he slept on ground
When he could have
 Anything he wished!

Was his act
A symbol of the fact
That we should always keep
Our feet on the ground
How much ever higher we fly?

Was he simply
Saluting the ground
On which he walked?

Or was it
A representation of the verity
That we are and shall remain
Nothing more than dust?

Or was it
A simple indication
That whatever one may become,
How much ever
Popularity, illustriousness and wealth
One may acquire;
One shall always
Disintegrate into dust?

I had a lot to learn that day
And as I walked back
I felt
That a little humility
Has also penetrated
Inside me!

Mithu Sen
New Delhi

MOU (Museum of Unbelongings): The Cabinets at my Home, New Delhi

Patron/Parent: Me, Mithu.
Area of Study: Anthropology of Emotions.
Motto: There is one for each one.

A personal archive of collected, received, stolen, inherited gifts, my home is the museum of these rarest of rare gifts. They define my life, my existence, my history. Left unacknowledged by many, these objects are actually part of everybody's life. They keep us aware of our roots, keep us rooted to the depths of our psyche.

The collection has piles of ordinary, unnoticed, unnecessary, abandoned, impermanent toys and unusual belongings, possessed by me and my children, with a passionate priority (and an obligation as well). They have been drawn together at a single point in time, entangled with each other in the same space and personalised by individual names.

A popular archive of cultural memory beyond the objects' historical identity. An unidentified deity who cannot be historicised, politicised- someone's talisman, another's personal fetish. A record of a life, a history of a vernacular culture and a symbolic archive of ephemeral impermanence.

The cabinets in my house are the museum of what does not belong to written history. They are the children of unrecorded past. And they have value much more than mere materiality. My child-centric attachment with the objects is personal and above any biological rites or familial obligations.

It is not a secret, neurotic engagement. Not self-centred, but self-seeking. Yet the idea is collective; inclusive as well as exclusive. This museum is open to all- people as well as their objects- easy to be identified with by any guest, with a promise to preserve personal histories, memories, moments.

These children are constantly in transit: looking for a new home, a new parent. They need love, affection and re-spect; and they spread the same around. Given with a smile, tended to with care, they teach us to acknowledge, what we, usually, overlook.

Gaurav Sharma
Bangalore, Karnataka

Ugly/Beauty: The Louvre, Paris, France

October 27th, 1983

'And here you are.'

Emma had finally found Alec.'I left you a note at the hotel reception' Alec replied his glance transfixed at the turban.

'The one mentioning about most ugly beauty,' Emma looked at the painting, 'and is this her?' she asked as she stood next to him.

'The Grande Odalisque' Alec murmured. 'The girl at reception mistook me as your wife' Emma said. 'See the contorted representation of her body,' Alec said, 'the gaze is mysterious and captivating but betrays no feeling.' If he had turned to see Emma he could've seen her eyes stuck at the details of the fabric rendered but he himself was too immersed in the painting.

'How can someone possibly call her anything but a masterpiece?' he said.

'Artists paint truth, lies, deceits, exaggeration, imaginations and fantasies.' Emma said as she broke out of the illusion.

She was amazed that she was sounding a pseudointellectual even to herself.

'Look around the works of Jacques-Louis David, an artist, a revolutionary, a dreamer, an opportunist, a nonconformist, the essential cog of Napoleon's propaganda machine but above all a true master.' Alec said as he pointed at the grand pieces of art around them.

'His convictions made the fanatic Marat a martyr, dying for a cause. He was the painter of Pope and the Emperor, the bard of Roman legends and a witness to the history in the making' he continued.

'Those were difficult times.' Emma said.

'And he swam through the changing political tides' Alec finished.

'You see this courtyard,' he pointed out from the window as they walked past it, 'some guy has great plans for it. He wants to build a hideous glass pyramid right here in midst of this classical architecture.' And after a momentary pause he added 'Sheer monstrosity.'

'Why would what is admirable in Egypt become hideous and ridiculous in Paris?' Emma said after some thought.

'What?' Alec was not sure what Emma meant.

'These are not my words.' Emma said, 'Gustave Eiffel replied that to the detractors of his Tower of Babel. Today who will consider Eiffel Tower as the dishonour of Paris? Clearly geniuses are recognised in retrospect.

Alec didn't say anything. Maybe he had nothing to say. Emma sensed that she had triumphed.

'What's next?' she asked casually.

'No. 779, Lisa Gherardini aka Mona Lisa,' Alec discounted his momentary loss, 'Come this way.'

Vatsala Sharma
New Delhi

Photographs: A Window to the Past and Memories: National Gallery of Modern Art, New Delhi

Nostalgia and memory are things that cause the most pleasure but at the same time the most pain.. Memories signify a thing in the past, and no matter what one can do, this past exists in the "past" and can no longer come into existence in the present. But that is exactly what makes it so beautiful. The only satisfaction that is accessible to one is to reminisce the past, and that holds the dissatisfaction too: the past can only be relived through memories. This creates a perpetual unsatisfiable desire to somehow step back in the good old days (even if those "good old days" had their faults) and meet the people, the conversations, the seasons, the music, the environment, the house, anything that makes up the past, and to just relive it just one more time. The melancholia, the nostalgia, becomes a poison but it is also a drought for some to somehow get through their present.

Photographs are a physical manifestation of a time captured, a memory, an experience captured forever. It captures not only a particular time and space, but also in a way the details, which though may seem irrelevant at that time, years later may function as various keys to build up the world of the past, of the memories. They are still irrelevant but provide a certain sense of comfort, a sense of illusion that yes, maybe this world does exist somewhere, even if it is now out of one's reach.

Sooni Taraporevala in her photo exhibition, Through a Lens, By a Mirror, The Parsis (1977-2013), captured and created a sense of timelessness and an overpowering sense of nostalgia. A melancholic air hangs over the works yet there is an aura of reminiscence. Taraporevala captures the various individuals of the Parsi community, engaged in routine activities, festivities, death, etc., and hence all the photographs seem to serve as shards of a broken mirror that Taraporevala strives to bring together by capturing them through the lens of her camera, reflecting her as well her community's identity and history.

Don't memories function in the same manner? Photographs seem a tangible form of these memories, of our past, but they are a mere reflection. Memories and photographs arouse these contradictory emotions, of joy yet sadness, of gains yet losses, of despair yet hope. One just has to live with the contradictions, and contradictions create art.

Aarushi Singh
Thane, Maharashtra

Curiousete: CSMVS, Fort, Mumbai

The wall was pastel green. The painting was gilt framed. It alone decorated the enormous wall. It alone consumed my attention and engaged my curiosity. Symphonies orchestrated by Vivaldi enthralled my inner ear as I observed and reflected on that old canvas sombre with meaning. The young girl was pretty in a red dress and a sobre bonnet with an eyepiece. The well, situated in the thick woods behind a summer house, interested this little girl and into the depths she peered with her ocular device. What was she looking for? Mysteries of the universe? Monsters? Lost secrets, perhaps? The well like an open mouth rising from the ground was furnished with riddles that the artist wouldn't reveal. She was at the same precipice at which Alice stood in front of the rabbit hole, the siblings who marched towards Narnia… every person who stands still and gazes out of the window of opportunity, contemplating. The artist conveys that same message as the girl peeks into that well of disasters or wonders. As the artist plays with deep greens, oak browns and the adorable red to show the tilt of the head, the setting of the scene and the initiation of the understanding of our diorama of unknown. The painting screamed at me to hold my nib and think what the unheralded painter meant when he painted the girl peeking into the well. Did he mean to motivate her to explore the well or just walk away? Did he mean to astonish her with treasures and dragons? Did he mean to inspire others to investigate their own worlds? What was so intriguing about that well? Ruminating on this, I felt that the painting beckoned me to devise and launch my own sail into the east wind. To chase myriad spectacles sewn by chaos and uncertainty. The artist knew well the inclination to know what happens behind closed doors, dark curtains and withdrawn souls. Perhaps that is why he left it at that pause, demanding us to examine our own wells.

Shanta Singha
Guwahati, Assam

She: Guwahati, Assam State Museum

Silent and grey it stares;
The sparkle is noticed.
I try to smile;
It smiles back at me –
Reminds me of the flakes.

As I sip my drink –
"Slurp , slurp.
It smiles and tells a story;
" I am a pretty young lass";
Black hair adorned with jasmines.
Love of his life that he created
Killed with hands.
The love died and he weeps.

Wonder do I?
He made you again-
Smiling yet silent and grey.

Unpropitious in love;
Why did she fall?
That's the story she tells
To all.

"Slurp, slurp";
My drink is over.
So as I move;
She smiles
And I step back;
I want to know more.

It says-
Dated 1310 AD
Sculptor and source – unknown.

Is that's all?
Her story is it?
She smiles at me;
She has noticed the sparkle;
She is silent and grey;
Thinks she who is me.

Shreya Sudesh
Chennai, Tamil Nadu

Of Light on Legacies: Egmore Museum, Chennai

Legends from far and beyond
Stand encased,
Sparking within us,
A deep curiosity

The smoothened edges of
The ruined Stone Sculptures
The Faded images of
Emperors who once ruled...

Bronze statuettes carved with
Ungodly intricacy stand
with impeccable poise
and shine with Ancient Grace.

The Light from the Clear-Storey
Windows above the ornate walls,
Falls upon their every facet and niche,
imparting shades and shadows.

Where this light illuminates
It also renders an uncommon depth
Bringing to life
every specimen, every relic.

Eras, Circa and Ages aplenty
All pass by our eyes in a jiffy,
loosening a barrage of thoughts

taking root in the essence of our intellect.
For the one who understands his Past,
Gets a hang on his present,
And the one who conquers this Avastha
Gets to claim His Future.

Glancing one last time at
The splendour of sparkling china
complementing the magnifique
Granite statues of Lambodhara...

We see that once
History's been written
No Era, No Religion, No Epic, No Nationality
has the might to part them...

As they coexist amidst one another
Under the same roof
Whispering Secrets of the Past
Into the On-lookers' ears.

A visit to the Museum,
Lights a million lamps of Iksenya
Awakens our inner hunger for Discovery
And introduces to us its idea of...Ekarthya.

....
Meanings : Avastha : Stage / Period
Lambodhara: Lord Ganesh
Iksenya: Curiosity
Ekarthya: Unity of an Idea

Sneha Sundaram
Mumbai, Maharashtra

The Weeping Woman: Tate Modern, London, UK

Her eyes bleed, Red
Realms of blood,
Coating my skin
Black Tears,
Piercing my soul.

I stare transfixed
As her eyes speak
Of the untold, oft seen
Horrors of war;
Images I run from daily,
Flashing before my eyes.

Of that desperate,
Crying man
Begging, pleading,
Tortured
Broken maybe for life.

Of streets littered
With limbs and blood
And maroon dust
That is afraid to rise,
Lest it be shot too.

I want to run away
But my feet are bound
In the weeping woman's spell.

Her pain my own
Her unheard cry
Echoing in my ears.

Maybe I'm in Guernica, like she was
Wanting to cowardly run away
Because, what words of comfort,
Can I give her?
She, who has lost so much?

Or am I in Bombay?
A scared little girl of 12
Running from a rioting mob?
No more, No more.
Too many, No more

The Tate is spinning.
The Azaan*, the church quire
And the temple bells,
Ring in the distance
Mingling with the loud
Roar of greedy wolves
Power, fame, money
War: Life as we know it today,
Or just something Picasso drew.

This poem is inspired by Picasso's "The Weeping Woman" that I saw at the Tate in London.
(*Azaan is the call to prayer from a Mosque)

Annie Besant Tresa Rani
Chennai, Tamil Nadu

Welcome to the Museum: The British Museum, London, UK

Welcome to the museum, madam. Pause on the threshold, sir. A few hours you will needto open Aladdin's cave of the past. What are you looking for, sir? What would you like to see, madam? A sarcophagus of glories past,or the enchantment of El Dorado's gold? Look, there stands our ancestor; clawed hands outstretchedtowards visions of an alien future. Can you tell in his eyes the dread of visions strange? Yes sir, this was us; this was you. The savage who became a manOr was it the man who embraced the savage? Will we ever know if he was nobler then or are we nobler now? Right this way, sir. Tread softly around that mummy, madam, lest we disturb Tutankhamen's dreams of Ankhesenamun. Ahh, ponder the rise and fall of civilisations. Wars, diseases and plagues that obliterate;innovation, beauty and art that commiserates. Human frailty, madam, found in these fragments and shells. The rise and fall of man and womanlike a leviathan breathing its last. Floundering in a morass of blood and glory. From this other side, you and I, would we have differed? See yesterday's boot print,sunk into stone, iron, bronze and steel; guns, machines, maps and flint; ships, gems, silk and spice. Do you not see in this museum? Man's play at being God. Do you not see in this museum? God's play at taming man? Thank you, sir. Goodbye, Madam. The clock tolls the closing hour. Let them rest now, these warriors brave,who survived history and give you courage to do the same.

IRELAND
Zoha Ahmed
Dublin

Vincent Van Gogh: The British Museum, London, UK

Red led to the rise of Passion,
Blue reduced it to due,
drops that fell through my eyes,
And then orange filled my view.

For a while it was fun until it too diluted to yellow,
So mellow, so mellow were the starry nights of violet,
that set my heart ablaze, the ashes of which came out
    green,
So mean, so mean life can be sometimes,
If only my mistakes could speak so they could mumble
    and teach me,
That the follies I commit need not be.

ITALY
Martin Bennett
Rome

'The Last of England': After a painting by Ford Madox Brown, Birmingham Museum & Art Gallery, Birmingham, UK

For Guglielmo and Valeria – Sicily-Australia

With two children (playful flaxen-haired girl;
Babe in arms, of whom one spies just the fingers)
He sits and sits, becoming his own statue,
Young wife trim and bonneted alongside,
Her umbrella raised against the worst
Either fortune of the elem ents might hurl.
Who knows what's in that fixity of gaze?
Behind them a grizzled compatriot
Spews curses at John bull, gabbles about
'Perfidious Albion', hopes which didn't turn out;
Then for bad measure shakes a belated fist.
The white cliffs of Dover loom smaller,
Smaller; waves to starboard, waves to larboard
Unleash a choppy discomforting green.
From the prow dangle vittles to last days
At most. Though the year's 1855
So many bluebirds've gone for a burton –
Through minor bankruptcy? Misdemeanour?
Then you have it, then you don't, one blow
Too far from the overweening skinflint,
Work? Upon such threads lives hang, sink, grow.

Pre-cheap flights, Eurozone, the Welfare State,
The globe is anything but their oyster.

His hat's more a helmet, brown overcoat
And buttons secretly shining armour
Now he's taken her tiny gloved hand
In his, its width gone bluish. She, in turn,
Gently cups the newborn's fingerends
And somewhere behind unblinking eyes, set mouth,
Envisages hard-pressed Mary and Joseph.
Given a Burne-Jones, her windswept scarf
Could be pink banderole, quixotic pennant;
Plain bonnet's a halo awaiting paint.
Lest myopically on their behalf
Rule some bleak-brained extraneous Fate,
He strengthens, meanwhile, his grip. No looking aft,
The die is cast. One age's emigrant
Is the next's refugee. Across hemispheres –
Come Finisterre or Cape of Good Hope –
Whichever end of history's telescope,
This is to wish them best of British –
For backup, that of the whole wide world.

NEW ZEALAND
Shih Yen Chang
Dunedin, Otago

Lotus Shoes: Otago Museum, Dunedin

At my local museum there is an exhibit of three pairs of brightly coloured lotus shoes. They look like tiny baby shoes, but were worn by Chinese women with bound feet. Every time I visit the museum, I am drawn to these shoes. I feel a connection to them because my maternal great-great grand-mother, who was born in the 1870s, had bound feet.

The ancient Chinese practice of foot binding began in the tenth century and continued for 1000 years. It was wide-spread during the Song Dynasty (960 - 1279 AD). Foot bind-ing started when girls were aged between 2 - 5 years old. Their feet were tightly bound with long pieces of cloth band-ages to stop their growth. This practice was excruciatingly painful because it deliberately broke the girls' toes and arch. Women with bound feet would never be able to run and could hardly walk.

The ideal goal in foot binding was to have feet as small as 3 inches (7.6cm) long. These were called 'golden lotus' because the tiny feet resembled a lotus bud. Feet that were 4 inches (10cm) long were also acceptable and were called 'silver lotus'. Women with bound feet wore shoes called 'three inch golden lotus shoes' (三寸金蓮鞋). These shoes were made of fabric, such as silk with cotton soles, and were always beautifully embroidered.

Ah, the price of beauty! Chinese women with bound feet could suffer deadly infections from foot binding. The bandages that bound the feet had to be changed and washed daily or at least a few times a week to prevent infections. Other problems included smelly and rotting flesh in the feet.

Foot binding was a status symbol. It was a symbol of beauty, wealth, elegance and even sexuality. Chinese women who wanted to marry well had to have bound feet as no one would marry a woman with large feet. Families who could bind the feet of their daughters were perceived as rich, because daughters with bound feet would never be able to work.

There were various unsuccessful attempts to ban foot binding in the 1800s and early 1900s. This practice took years to die out. The last factory in China that made shoes for bound feet finally closed in the late 1990s. Nowadays, lotus shoes can only be seen in museums. They are from a bygone era, a relic of the past.

NIGERIA
Emecheta Christian
Makurdi, Benue State

The Museum: National Gallery of Modern Art, Lagos

I still remember that awesome day like the name of my
father
It was on a first of October when I set foot on that palace
of histories reminder

It was like every normal house but it embodied in it the
life and soul of our dying past
Revealing hidden realities and debunking with visible
facts things we once knew as fantasy and mystery

Browsing through the photo collage of our heroes past I
felt their zeal and unyielding will staring me right in the
eyeball
And a voice of repute and honour speaking loud in my
head saying I shouldn't let the struggles of our heroes past
fall

My sight blazed in awe at the original statues and heads
of traditional gods which we once played with as kids
And I wonder who stripped them of their powers because
everyone probably heard stories of their great deeds

Looking to the left I see a painting which speaks our past,
present and future
To me this painting was more of magic than painting
existing within the four corners of a framed picture

Night was fast approaching and I knew it was time to retire
On leaving the museum, a fire in me was ignited and something within me was grateful to God for being inspired.

Francis Ugochukwu Maduakor
Awka, Anambra

Gloom: National War Museum, Umuahia

"That Ogbunigwe, the cylindrical locally made weapon we saw in the museum, killed people in thousands like the Boko Haram bombs; salt deficiency, kwashiorkor, hunger, famine roasted people alive in Biafran War." Papa shook his head, as his scaly lips, swayed up and down like a see-saw, when he talked. My eyes were wet, soaked with tears, tears that hung tenaciously like the national green and white flag on the tall flagpole at the National War Museum, Umuahia, tears that never rolled down. My hands were wet too on the car steering wheel on the road back from the museum and there were sweats under my breasts and my armpits; and Papa's legs were white, dusty from the harmattan like his grey hairs.

"Soldiers, with black paint, charcoal over their faces and green leaves on their heads, just like those statues and pictures in the museum, pursued us from our village." I was still trying to picture the soldiers with long guns and knives, breaking mud houses, thatch-roofed, women with their babies on their back running, when Papa said "She was killed during our flew, it was so difficult running around, with you, only three years old then, your brother and your pregnant mother like ijiji, houseflies." Papa gave a heavy breathe; heavy tensions crawled away, through his nostrils, his nostrils that were wide and resembled two sewage pipes. And the grimace on his face made him look like Okey, my son, when he is sad.

"Those soldiers, heartless, came closer, I ran away with you and your brother, they captured your mother, her pregnancy made weak to run." Papa's eyes were still creamy gloss like the yoghurts, Udonna, my elder brother brought back from the U. K when he visited last Christmas, but his voice sound feeble.

"I hid in the bush, they all had long knives, that type we saw in the museum, the tied your mother to an orange tree, I still remembered her wails, louder when the thorns pricked her, my heart melted, I sobbed quietly, and with their knives, they cut her belly, until they pulled out the red bloody foetus and chopped off the eriri-nwa, placenta, she died slowly." Papa stopped. His weak voice ceased.

I never knew the loud sob was mine, until I turned and saw tears running down Papa's eyes.

Ubio Obu
Calabar, Cross River

The Last Drum of Freedom: Slave Trade Museum, Marina Resorts, Calabar

This drum sounded a long time ago
And was why we left our bed forego
It reminded us that nothing's so sweet
like our ego
And to fight; ergo.

Ta-ta-ta-ta-ta-ta the drum began
Suddenly we became aware we were
on chains
And that the tears on our eyes were due
to pains
We could see the shackles all around us
We suddenly realised what we loosed
Just then, the streets started boiling
Men started chanting
Women supporting
Children yelling
We could hear the smell of freedom
The savours of freedom
The fragrance of freedom
We could glance ahead and see freedom
Oh how sweet freedom looks
Freedom must come into African Kingdom.

Kpra-kpra-kpra the drum continued
With guns and sword we all queued
Time for freedom has surely cued

We were set to change all that was
skewed
The air settled the precedence
Our streams were looking so deadly
The lakes and rivers gave us our
temerity
The rocks and mountains were
whispering, be very shoddy
No wonder why we were so, so, screwy.

Kpam-kpam-kpam-kpam the drum
resounded
And I could see the ointment of freedom
flowing from our bodies
The bitter taste of colonisation had made
us fester and fettered
Our saliva's turned to blood
Our blood turned to bile
Our eyes turned red
while our hearts blackened
Here we started revolting
Their orders we snared
Their stripes we returned
Their laws we no more submitted
Their decree we never subjected
We better die in freedom than lye in
bondage
Just then, we heard the last drum of
freedom.

KPOM! KPOM! KPOM! KPOM!
The last drum of freedom echoed
We became conscious, curious, vicious
and ferocious
We fought with all strength and vigour
With all amount of alacrity we fought

without pity
At this time, all we could hear was
freedom echoing
All we could feel was the breeze of
freedom blowing
All we could see was signals of
freedom coming
As we fought, many were dying
But this rather fostered us to keep trying
We tried, tried, finally we eyed
Freedom descending like a dove
Oh freedom, Freedom at last.
We started singing, but songs of freedom
We started clapping, but claps of
freedom
Oh how beautiful freedom looked that
fateful day
She was dressed in beads
She was dazzling and shining
Her smile so glamorous
We all embraced freedom
We could feel her warmth
freedom at last!

PAKISTAN
Ariba Zahir
Karachi, Sindh

Of Massive Wings, Metallic Bodies And Mechanical Birds...:PAF Museum Karachi, Shahra-e-Faisal

At the age of ten, my father drove us to a museum of airplanes.

I was very excited for my first visit to a museum. My father and my younger brother were both crazy about airplanes while I just wanted to see a museum. As we walked towards the museum, my father would occasionally talk about a random airplane and call it by some difficult name; all I imagined was a big plane, a small plane, a long plane...

Once we entered the museum, I was in awe. The museum was very big with planes everywhere: airplanes on my right, airplanes on my left, airplanes up front, airplanes hanging off walls... Apart from airplanes, there were also plastic dummies wearing different clothes and symbols on the walls of various air force related stuff. However, the planes had caught my attention. I did not even know what fascinated me about them - the feeling was unknown to me.

Throughout the visit, I did nothing but gazed at those huge flying objects...

"Keep looking up... That's the secret of life." – Snoopy

At the age of fifteen, my father drove us to the Pakistan Air Force Museum.

My family decided to spend a day out together so we visited the air force museum. The shared passion about airplanes was still evident in the eyes of my father and brother. The museum remained the same, from both the outside and the inside. The airplanes were not a day old, the mannequins were properly dressed in their respective uniforms and various air force emblems and photos of the past still decorated the white walls. Nothing had changed – not even my excitement.

Father would stop in front of airplanes and eagerly tell their names: Shenyang F-6 Aircraft, Vickers VC.1 Viking, Folland Gnat… As for me, I just stared at the airplanes – standing so still; undeterred; back straight; looking up; looking ahead; so focused… They had my complete attention.

The same feeling came back from five years ago and tugged at my heart. Although, this time, I could describe it clearly: the feeling was to be determined; the feeling was to look ahead and stay focused, no matter what; the feeling was to keep your back straight and be confident; the feeling… the feeling was overwhelming. Just like airplanes, I wanted to touch the skies.

Those massive-winged, metallic bodied, mechanical birds had inspired me…

RUSSIA
Katherine Turkina
Belgorod, Belgorod region

Blank Verse of Shadow Theatre. K. Malevich "Black Square":The State Tretyakov Gallery, Moscow

Blank verse of melancholy.
Black garden.
Emptiness and lines.
Square.

Red corner. View chained
To the wall.
Cup hit
In wine.

Frame of the twenty-fifth.
The Reserves. Installation.
Scaffold cursed.
Hype.

Fatal flight.
Canvas blank.
Shot. Someone behind the screen.
Live.

SERBIA
Milan Simonovic
Belgrade

When My Dream Comes True: Narodni Muzej, Belgrade

As I walk through the city's heart, there you stand. Behind the monument of the man who laid your foundations. This man, lucky you, was the head of the state at that time and wanted to enlighten its own people with knowledge that you should hold.

Since then ages have passed by, wars, rulers, many generations have been blessed to see you from the inside. But now, for at least ten years your main doors are shut. Once the great jewel in the crown of the nation, you've become a dirty rock in the city's main centre. Yes, you still are beautiful from the inside, and you still hold many valuable evidence of the art and kind of the people who live or have lived here. But you are closed for the outside world of the 21st century.

I watched you carefully as I grew up to become a student, and since my first walking steps I wanted to see what that dusty building of yours has inside. But now, where they were once brown, they are now covered in black dust and ash, doors that are closed. And are yours.

Your face has been covered with black fumes from passing cars and traffic, and all other buildings around you seem to be ashamed of your looks. I am ashamed to see you like that. I now walk without help of my parents, and still want to see what you are keeping inside. You have an entrance on the side, but it's not the entry you expect the main museum in the country to have.

I was delighted when I saw the workers erecting the platform for restoration, and I danced like nuts saying: "My dream is coming true." But it didn't last for long. Like some linked lifeline your faith is remarkably the same with the faith of the people that walk near you.

You are full of wonders inside, but closed like you don't believe anyone. You are ill, sick and full of wounds (your roof can't keep the rain out). You think you're left alone... but no, you're wrong.

For the good of other kids that see you with great eyes full of dreams, as I once was, I will not rest until I see you shining like a star on the clear night sky.

On the day when my dream comes true.

SINGAPORE
Yu Ching Tan
Singapore

Glass Changes: National Museum of Singapore

We established that hearts,
those wild, savage creatures,
slid themselves between the crevices
of our ribs,
and caged themselves in.

Remember cages. Remember sometimes
they are meant to keep things in.
Realise that other times,
they exist to keep things out.
Remember, remember.

See those swords in glass cages?
Watch them slowly narrate
stories, smell the metal rust in the air,
then think of blood and sweat and white flags.
White flags are why this museum exists.

"This man died defending his country."
But no, no, I say.
He is no patriot,
this man died because there was
something he loved more than himself.

"Despite being weaker, we won this war."
but no, no, I say. Again.

See those swords?
These swords have taken more sons than Death,
(and parents should not watch their children die).

I look again. These cages are meant to
keep things in. The swords are safe,
they will no longer be fierce feral blood-drainers.
The swords are safe.
And so are our sons.

SRI LANKA
Rossana Favero-Karunaratna
Depanama, Pannipitiya

That Small Museum!: Yatala

In July, 2011 I had the opportunity to visit a small museum next to the remains of the Yatala Dagaba in Sri Lanka. The museum was just a simple room with a number of rare antiquities displayed in specific order. The person in charge was a humble man, Mr Prematilleke, who seemed to be extremely happy to see visitors. I wondered how many people had actually visited the place and decided to ask about it. The old man just smiled and referred to be part of a place "known by the word of mouth". I was just thinking how this place could be called a "museum" when suddenly I was taken to a marvellous place, 2300 years back in history. Mr Prematilleke dedicated almost two hours to enthusiastically share his knowledge with us and gave life to every piece found there.

Two months after my visit the museum would be robbed and a large Buddha statue taken away in order to find some precious gems supposedly hidden inside it. I felt so bad about it that I decided to go back with my family. When I got there Mr Prematilleke greeted me warmly but warned me I could not enter because of the repairs needed to be made after the attack. However he was able to give us good news: the statue had been recovered and the perpetrators arrested. The media coverage finally granted the museum greater support and recently a foreign Embassy got involved in improving the conditions of the place. The museum was restored and now features greater security facilities.

I am planning to pay a visit to the Yatala Museum- now described as small and modern- to see all this improvement, but most of all I hope to meet Mr Prematilleke once again. These events have made me realize what an inspiring museum is all about. I was not only inspired to know more about the place, the artefacts, the people who lived at that time and their relevance, but the importance to keep museums alive. They rely on the passion to understand the past and transport it to the present, making it available for anyone who simply wants to be part of this adventure. We don't need gigantic structures for a museum to become inspiring but to realise the role that people like Mr Prematilleke play.

He made that small museum certainly inspiring.

SWIZERLAND
Elsa Fischer
Bern

The Old Masters: "Still Life" Exhibit. - Kunstmuseum, Basel 2009

The Old Masters

were not afraid of death:

its cold light reflected on the skull,

the withered ears of rye, a toppled rummer,

the book now closed. The dice are cast

the candle dies.

I turn away from rotting fish on Delft Blue,

the stained fruit, the fly, the maggot.

Outside, a dog sniffs out the living

who wait to enter. Through the exit

go those who've seen what soon they'll be.

Who queue to pay for postcards.

(e r i s q u o d s u m)

UKRAINE
Antonina Litak
Uzhhorod District, Transcarpathian Region

We Are All Leaves Of The Same Tree: The Museum of Folk Architecture and Life, Uzhhorod

Have you ever pondered
On the essence of living and life
Inside the moment of the past arrested?
Do we resemble bees in a giant hive?
By next generations let's not be detested...

Children of civilisation...Nothing seems to be able to impress us. In the summertime roaming about the city in search of novel ideas, some mighty forces of light led me to the picturesque southern slope of Castle Hill, upon which one of the first Ukrainian open-air museums of Folk Architecture and Life is situated. The Transcarpathian Museum of Folk Architecture and Life is found in the ancient historical part of the city, behind the premises of the Castle. The monuments of architecture of the late 18th – early 20th centuries comprise 7 homesteads, 6 dwellings, a church, a blacksmith, a watermill, a fullery, a tavern, a schoolhouse built of wood. Over 14 thousand objects are kept in the museum. While scrutinising the exhibits does anyone realise that formerly, being deprived of any special equipment, machines, computers, people managed to create such things? Every single object radiates the warmth of human hands, a piece of the craftsman's soul is believed to have remained in it. This fact underscores the importance of a human being as a creator, not a profiteer.

Stop for a while. Look around. Buildings erected here and there are higher, more luxurious than they used to be. Today people's mode of life is wasteful. The spirit of hatred, envy, rivalry, greed is in the air. Involuntarily, start thinking that the humankind has lost measure in everything: lack of it gives rise to ubiquitous chaos. Being immoderate, we are doomed. In the society which is debilitated by multifaceted disorder and narrow-mindedness, wars are launched. Having changed priorities, we are thoughtlessly destroying our nature by enormous consuming. We forget that being a part of the nature, which is the basis of life itself, we are vanishing as a biological species and race.

It is the energetics of lively and harmonious interrelations of a man and his environment that makes the essence of folk creative work as well as that of life in general. It must be this energy that has been attracting visitors for many years, making them aware of the significant fact – we are all leaves of the same tree.

Alla Vovk
Kiev

Kiev, Independence Square

I never thought that Museum would be a museum for the whole city. The last four months in Kiev there are things that whole world is watching for them. I remember when we were evacuated from the University during the evening classes. It was impossible to get home to the other bank of the Dnieper. Underground was mined, public transport worked with big problems. Columns of people walked. In this time on the Maidan in cold weather, people assembled cobblestone barricades. After the events of the end of February the city was quite different: flowers at the portraits of the dead, bullets, Berkuts Weapons Museum (they were shooting at people), tents, tears. Blood shed for the future of my children. At first I wanted to write about one of the art galleries that inspires me, return to the past and forward thinking, but now my city is imbued with freedom, the spirit that rules me and thousands of people. When people die in Kiev, but do not back down from the barricades when they are ready to fight to end the corrupt machine power, to fight and die for their freedom, you know that there is true democracy and the true will of the people. Everyone got a chance to be a little bit better and finally feel part of a single body, whole and mighty and in this revolution. The fact that we got a chance to rebuild their society, which we will learn to love and respect. Both politicians and the authorities have nothing to do with it, the nation did it itself, without foreign forces. This is our great victory, which we can really be proud of. More than 20 years ago, Ukraine gained its independence thanks to a handful of patriots and with historical luck. No formal paragraphs of laws and resolutions, but breathing life and force to millions of citizens who are prepared to fight for their country. All the sacrifices during these months by heroes throughout Ukraine, were not in vain, our common sacred duty now is to build this new, free, fair and prosperous Ukraine. I hope and believe in my future museum. Future of our country.

UK
Kenneth Adams
Thornton-Cleveleys, Lancashire

Inspired By My Museum: Fleetwood Museum, Lancashire

My museum is in Fleetwood, where the Council used to
meet
And if I listen carefully, I hear the sound of marching feet
Of soldiers, from the barracks, as they go to board the
train
To take them to the trenches, to the mud, the gas, the
pain.
For the station stood across the way until the line was
shut
And a stately building was removed, an artery was cut.
The Isle of Man boats followed, and then the fishing fleet
And Fleetwood had to find a way to get back on its feet.

Now I hear the "Pilling Pig" as bold as you can find
Carrying along the single track the salt so newly mined.
Taking it off to Glasson Dock, or to the I.C.I.
Up river with its chimney burning gases in the sky.

The sounds all change when darkness falls, I listen then
with care
As railway workers in the yards shunt noisy wagons
there.
And the bucket dredger in the channel starts to clank and
wail
As it works to stop the build up upon the 'Tiger's Tail'.
Still listening – I can hear it, the "cock-a-doodle-do"

Of trawler sirens leaving port, to fish for me and you.
Or trawlers corning on the tide, inward, by the score.
And wives all shouting greetings as they pass along the
shore.

Stood on the steps, looking right, and Dock Street I can
see
Where workers toil to feed the ships, a real fishing family
Trawlers' Supply and Gourock Ropes, descriptive names
like this
Great Grimsby Coal Salt and Iron Co - oh what utter
bliss!
Still on the steps, but looking left, see the ferry to Knott
End
And then the lifeboat slipway, further round the bend
I see the Fleetwood lighthouse as I look straight out to sea
But in this town, as you might guess, it's only one of
three!

And I feel the Fleetwood spirit, of its people, of its dock
Of its trams and pubs and cycles, and its four faced lying
clock.
Its prawners on the Jubilee, the sail boats carrying logs
The early morning lumpers, streets echoing to their clogs
Its fish and chips and mussels, kippers you can send
Its world renowned throat lozenge called "The
Fisherman's Friend"
And all this information, and much - oh, so much, more
Is available to all who walk through my museum's door.

Robert Awork
Liverpool, Merseyside

My Daughter and the Museum: Liverpool Museum

Our encounter with the Museum of Liverpool is a life-changing experience, a realisation of the past, an inspiration. My Daughter & I have visited the Museum, for the past 3 years, since she was born and able to go out of the house. I have always chosen this place for inspiration and entertainment. There have been times when, having no money or just enough to get the bus into town for something to do, the Museum is the only free activity in the City that is warm and welcoming. Always with some activity that we can take home or just a new exhibit which inspires or creates awe in her little eyes. This alone has been a rewarding experience when visiting the Museum. She now is almost five and asks regularly of a weekend can we go to the Museum, which we do...

Father and Daughter while Mum rests, use the City's Museum. Cause daughter thinks it's the best, it has Fish, Egypt, African masks, Indian head dresses, and activity tasks. It has big dinosaurs, Roman and International Art and something on the top floor that's to do with stars. It has exhibitions of missions that happened long ago. Daughter asks questions, I know most things daughter. But there some things that I just do not know. We read the programme, we follow the leads, we get distracted by African beads. We see the mummies in tombs, monkeys, baboons. We hear Canadian story and Inuit tunes. We play games of ships that have travelled the world, Daddy can I work in the Museum as a girl? Of course my love. She goes off down the corridor and does her own twirl. There is space for a run, her little short legs. The more that we come, the more that she gets. She knows people used different tools in the past, and how whales grew large. How some chicks hatched, way, way long ago. The more we visit the more she knows.

We are poor, not much money to spare, we have joy, we have pride, we have love and care. We have bus fare and sandwiches, but no money to spare. But when we land in the museum, we stand and just stare. The pterodactyl at the entrance is sight to be seen, it chases my daughter but only in dreams.

Peter Barnfather
Shrewsbury, Shropshire

Reflections: Musée du Louvre, Paris, France

A small girl tentatively approaches a painting. Noticing its name plate she runs her fingers under the text and reads it aloud, 'Interior of a Collector's Cabinet.' Her eyes move to the painting, an apparent reflection of the walled art encapsulating her tiny frame; a mirror to this painted vault.

After a short while gazing she is certain of a change, that something before her is not as it was. 'Those figures have moved,' she points to a group in the foreground of the painting, but no one is paying her any attention. She blinks and rubs her eyes, realising she must be imagining it. Moving closer she notices a delicate noise, a rustling of fabrics. She leans in closer still, becoming lost in her surroundings and now not entirely certain of anything. She begins to notice the smallest things; the freshness of the drying canvases, the crisp Belgian air from the landscape outside, her senses swirling as if freed. Her attention is drawn to the smallest of details; she giggles at the attentive dog and his proud master, gasps at the brightness of the parrot's feathers, and cranes her neck to take in the sheer scope of the vaulted room before her. She does not blink, she is too enraptured by the experience, taken by the image before her.

A moment passes. As her mother takes her by the hand the girl blinks and has returned.

Skye Bayley
Stoke on Trent, Staffordshire

Trapped: Potteries Museum and Art Gallery, Stoke on Trent

Being forced to work in a museum was Boring, yes the capital B was needed, I happened to have the pleasure of working there all day. My mum is a cleaner there and she broke her leg and couldn't go to work, fortunately it was the summer so there was no school and lucky me got to replace her for the next 3 weeks -frankly I couldn't wait... to leave.

My dad wouldn't let me get out of it, in fact the wonderful man insisted on driving me there and escorting me inside.

Shuffling to the desk as slowly as possible, I looked up and saw a woman around 30 with one of those smiles that never leave your face, no matter how annoyed you get. She told me my shift was in the art gallery and basically my job was to stand there all day waiting for some cheeky cod to throw a wrapper on the floor.

The Art Gallery was on the top floor, and because of my weird lift phobia, stairs were the only option. I have never liked art at all, it bored me to tears, so standing in the middle of a room with no purpose at all was just the last thing I wanted to be doing on a Friday. I kept watching the clock, wandering round. Every minute felt like a lifetime! To pass the time I decided to look at some of the paintings give art a chance, all were boring except for just one.

In the darkest corner was a painting, of a forest, it looked so real, trees all over, and a river running through the middle and mountains in the back dusted with snow.

Looking closer between the trees was a face, a girl peeking out through a gap in the trees, I edged closer, so close I had to squint to focus, there was something familiar about that face, something that made the hair on the back of my neck stand on end, then it hit me, it was familiar because it was me!

I was in the painting the same curious eyes and straight nose and dark wavy hair.

I needed air, I quickly walked to the door to the stairs and pulled it open and I found myself peeking out between two trees.

I was literally in the painting and I had to get out, fast.

Sarah Beney
Croydon, Surrey

Remembrance: RAF Air Defence Radar Museum, Neatishead, Norfolk

I visited The Royal Air Force Air Defence Radar Museum on 23/07/13. It was an unexpected day out as due to rain, my partner, his mother and I had to cancel our original plans.

I was very ignorant about the Royal Air Force and knew nothing about them until my visit. My Grandad served in the Army and my Auntie has served in the Navy but I had no connection to the RAF.

The day I visited the museum, there was no-one else waiting for the tour so the three of us were guided around the museum, just ourselves and the various volunteer tour guides which enabled us to have lots of time to look, listen and ask questions.

The items I saw, the articles I read and the stories I heard whilst touring around the museum moved me to tears. I realised I had been very naive about the importance of the Royal Air Force and was ashamed of myself.

The day had such an emotional impact on me that I felt compelled to write the following poem:

There are things that we've not been part of.
We're fortunate not to have been.
Without the men and women who died for us,
Our lives wouldn't be so serene.

There were heroes on land and at sea,
Flying high up in the sky too,
Giving their lives for you and for me
And for our friends and families too.

These people should not be forgotten,
Their bravery should be well known,
For not once did they think of themselves.
They fought for Britain, their home.

Anna Berg
Wigan, Lancashire

The Teacher Smiled: Imperial War Museum North, Manchester

Are we
There yet miss
Can I eat crisps
Is there a gift shop
(For my mum)
Are we
Lining up outside miss
Can I get a latte
We all need the loo
(Our mascara's run)
Are we
Doing work here miss
I'm missing games
Jordan's writing in pink
(On his hand)
Are we
Listening to her miss
Can I go out
I've got a toilet pass
(Need a cig).
Are we
Holding a real one miss
Can I touch it next
Will it go off
(Secretly hoping)

Feeling the weight

they were people like you
Too young to grasp?
These objects that echo

We are
Leaving school
Pals together
Joking to France
(Miss they lied)
We are
Hefting a shell
Emptying boots
Writing a letter
(Miss they were in love but He couldn't tell her)
We are
Discarding teenagers
For forty minutes
Nothing is written
(But a lot is said)

Are we
Going now miss
Can we keep the grenade
John's in the toilet
(His brother's abroad).

Are we
Tidying the coach miss
Can I open my crisps
It's quiet isn't it
(For ten minutes)
Are we
Nearly there miss
Can I get dropped off here
I'm knackered, me
(Emotional wormhole)
We are

Back in our now
Gadgets off silent
Backpacks slung

(Thanks miss).

Rachel Bourne
Telford, Shropshire

The Bigger Picture: Herbert Art Gallery and Museum, Coventry

(Inspired by the Quentin Blake Exhibition 'As Large as Life')

In a world where the relevance of The Arts is often questioned
And children can be discouraged to study 'such things' at school,
It enthuses me to see that Art can set you free
And the proof is plastered here upon these walls.

Blake has used his talent over decades
To entertain, enlighten and enthuse.
His inspiring approach to Art, featuring in novels with real heart,
Has encouraged many to make their dreams come true.

Here Art expresses what our elders feel,
In 'Our Friends in the Circus' their wishes become real.
From breathing clouds of fire to juggling higher and higher,
Their bodies show their memories are as strong as a tightrope wire.

Then onto the simply named 'Ordinary life',
Created for those who find eating a great strife.
A painting full of hope, for those who thought they were broke,
Shows they will achieve these things, now Art has given them wings.

So, in a world where the relevance of The Arts is often
questioned
This exhibition is a huge breath of fresh air.
It proves that Art can be a kind of therapy
To ensure the bigger picture is always there.

Becky Bye
Shaftesbury, Dorset

The Museum: Sturminster Newton Museum, North Dorset

Shattered remains reside,
Gathering dust.

Memories whispering
Trapped in cases,

Time trickling like the sands.

Echoes running through corridors,
Casting across paintings
Shadows creeping over forgotten relics.

Terry Caffrey
Warrington, Cheshire

Glass I: St. Helen's Glass Museum, Merseyside

The blow pipe kiss of life shapes the molten sun,
rotating, like a Kaleidoscope along the cool marver,
feeding the hungry Glory Hole while glass is finely spun.

Sand, lime, soda, fired the bottle neck's last run,
London gherkin shaped into the sky erupts, volcanic larva.
Transparency fused, now the silicate's job is done.

Glass to stop the bullet and bottle feed the sun,
to stem the flood, cap the fizz codswollop, and drunken palaver.
Feeding the hungry Glory Hole while glass is finely spun.

Mirror, 300BC and Rome, when recycling had begun
hushed stained glass cathedrals, befitting of the Father.
Transparency fused, now the silicate's job is done.

Reflections of our past, our bottled future is not undone.
Perfume, sauce, medicine and pints of gassy lager.
Feeding the hungry Glory Hole while glass is finely spun.

Crystal clear chandelier, furnaced one to one.
Beauty in the Le Louvre pyramid, classy rainbow carver.
Transparency fused, now the silicate's job is done.
Feeding the hungry Glory Hole while glass is finely spun.

The style of poem is a Villanelle.
Marver is the bench used by a glass blower
The Glory Hole is part of the furnace.
Codswollop was the first glass bottle with a glass stopper ever made.

Andrew Campbell-Kearsey
Brighton, East Sussex

The Brighton Museum Cat: Brighton Museum, East Sussex

We all wrote about the cat and which rubber we'd bought. Our poor teacher had visited Brighton Museum in advance and slavishly prepared the copious worksheets for our trip. I seem to recall the focus should have been an exhibition about textiles and their manufacture.

But when we came to write up our visit the following week the cat's qualities and attributes had increased in magnitude in our collective child's memory.

'It had stripes.'

'No it didn't. It was ginger.'

The key facts we agreed on was that the cat was a willing repository for our loose change. We'd greedily fed the papier-mâché cat model with coins through a small slit in its chest. It stood taller than us, and in gratitude it purred and its eyes lit up for a brief second. It was magical. We'd been eager for our next fix and jostled with each other to make the next payment, just to hear that transitory purr of aloof satisfaction.

The teacher caved in and our classroom was covered with a bewildering array of feline illustrations. No paisley prints, looms or spinning jennies graced the walls. It was strange how the thirty children had visited the same museum, yet our recall of the cat varied so widely.
*****

I'd moved to London for my first job. On the spur of the moment I'd asked somebody out from work. She'd agreed and after a couple of dates, I'd suggested a weekend away. I think there was a flicker of disappointment in her eyes when I hadn't mentioned Venice or Paris. But as interns, money was tight.

On the train trip to Brighton, I thought of where I'd take her and hoped I'd bump into the right people, friends who'd show me in a good light. On the Saturday afternoon we walked through the Pavilion Gardens and I saw the entrance for the revamped museum, all glass and light. We looked around. She wanted a coffee but I wouldn't have been satisfied until I'd been in every room. Surely they hadn't pensioned off the cat. I couldn't believe I was old enough to succumb to nostalgia. I was only twenty-three.

The shop was unsurprisingly situated just in front of the exit. Then I spotted the cat. It was so small. It didn't purr or light up. It just accepted money.

It's true: Never go back.

Jane Campion Hoye
Sutton Coldfield, West Midlands

Waterfall Glory: The Guinness Storehouse Museum, Dublin, Ireland

Drop by tiny drop they gather,
Clad in their robes of high mountain purity,
Sanctified by the high crosses and stone circles
Of ancient monasteries,
Threading down through mysterious mountains,
Gathering speed from secluded lakes,
Tumbling into ragging rivers,
Weaving beside the hidden tracks
Of the county that's known
As the Garden of Ireland.

Here they come, fresh for their mission,
These multitudinous water pilgrims,
Hammering the railings of the Museum,
Flooding the sluices of the Storehouse,
Pounding in armies over the heads
Of those who stand in St James' Gate,
Staring up as they make
The ultimate sacrifice.

In sheet after shimmering sheet they plunge,
Submitting their souls in glorious surrender,
As rotating paddles and scalding hot cylinders
Bubble and boil and mash their liquor
Of chaste, clear, mountainous water
Into the wort of hops and barley
That slowly transfigures into a sea
Of pure liquid ebony.

And 'Cheers' is the toast as we sip and savour
The newborn brew on the tasting floor.
Then 'Cheers' again as we raise a glass
In the bar of the brewery's skyline tower,
Surveying, like gods,
The rooftops of Dublin,
Declaring, like priests,
The travellers' blessing:
'May the road
Always rise up to meet you'.

Glynis Charlton
Bingley, West Yorkshire

Krill: Maritime Museum, Hull

Leaning closer to the jar, I study
the suspended writhe of you. Gathered
from a bottle nosed whale, stoppered
in your death year; now placed on this shelf
beside oilskin and scrimshaw.
Jostling around me, the Year 9 boys,
eager, shoving, wanting to know:
Miss, is it brains?

We imagine your story, picture the deck,
thousand upon thousand of you,
bucketing from that cavernous mouth,
swabbing spiked boots of the heaving men
who harpooned and butchered;
and then – somehow – landing here,
in this dusty half light. All that remains
of a whale that did not even taste you.

Lynda Clark
Nottingham

Climbing Stairs in Karlsruhe: Badisches Landemuseum, Karlsruhe, Germany

"There's nothing there!" Every German I meet en route protests. "Why would you go there?!"

It's true that had an old school friend not lived here, it's unlikely I would have come to Karlsruhe. Which makes me feel fortunate she does live here.

Being museum geeks, one of the first things we do is visit the palace that gives Karlsruhe its name – Karl's Ruhe. Or Karl's Peace, a name Karl Wilhelm apparently came up with when lounging under a tree. 18th Century Margraves, eh?

It's an impressive white building with a tall domed tower. The grounds are immaculate, two gardeners working their way across the vast lawns on mowers as we pass, filling the air with the scent of fresh cut grass.

Karl certainly didn't do anything by halves. His house is enormous. From bottom to top, the palace's museum tells the story of Baden-Wurttemberg (the state Karlsruhe's at the centre of) through the ages, incorporating art, culture and religion. All information is in German, but the vast majority of displays are either fascinating in their own right, or self-explanatory. My friend's reasonable level of fluency gets us through the rest.

After a brief conversation with a curator, my friend 'thinks' she knows how to get to the tower. With views of Karlsruhe's famed concentric layout, she's keen not to miss out, leading us through what I'm convinced is a fire exit. We climb flight after flight of stairs, passing offices and storage rooms and I prepare my "I told you so's" for when we're found and thrown out. My legs are soon turned to jelly and I curse Karl's architectural preferences all the way to the top, muttering; "Karl, would it have killed you to install a lift?!"

But no-one throws us out and, exhausted, we finally reach the tower's apex. I'm forced to pause for a moment while my legs solidify again, temporarily tentative about their ability to hold my weight.

I'm neither good with heights nor fond of exercise, but as I peer into gardens with swimming pools; as I look out across the trees and rooftops, radiating outwards like the ripples from a pebble dropped into a still pond; as I enjoy a view very similar to the one Karl must have enjoyed all those years ago, I'm very glad he didn't skimp on the stairs.

Phoebe Clothier
Windsor, Berkshire

The Will To Survive: Imperial War Museum, London

The hooves of the horses clapped on the ground,
The grunting, the scuffling broke the silence around,
In went the spurs, up went the call,
The fearing and rearing and killing of war.
Shells shot themselves from enemy guns,
The men on each side looked to the blood of the sun,
The horses rebelled but were forced to the push,
Limbs, guns, bodies hung from the tree and the bush.
The air was of blood; prayers mixed with curse,
The training and practice were no means of rehearse,
Splattering, spluttering, dead on the floor,
The rest of the men staring at Death and his door.
War is a fever, the crackle of powder,
War is a life under enemy shower,
But one sense was there, with a hope to revive,
And that was the hope and the will to survive.

Oran Crawford
Bangor, Co Down, Northern Ireland

The day I met Evil: Auschwitz-Birkenau, Poland

I walk through the cobbled streets, looking up at the many bars on the windows, the dust crunching under my sole, like many others who walked this path for the last time. I get to go home. I feel so drained as we walk up to the building, which so many men called home. They truly had nothing. Walking between the rooms, the many pictures of the faceless men and women seem to follow me. How men can do such evil is beyond me. I struggle up the many worn brick stairs. Before we walk into the room, we are told "no photographs and this is not a necessary part of tour". We walk through a sick and twisted room with a wall of human hair. I could deal with that but the next room I wish I never entered. Laid before me is a row of baby shoes, clothes and even toys. I can't take it, eyes stinging, throat raw, I run outside and sit on the curb. I look across the hill to a small grey building. How many died there? How many knew what was happening? Why did nobody care? I'm sitting in a graveyard. Died from natural causes, sickness, riot. All lies, just so they could kill innocent people. My small world of safety, happiness and compassion came crashing down on me. Why is the museum there? So history doesn't repeat itself. So we can remember, not their crime but how low humanity can dip. The most important reason it is there, so we see evil but also remember evil never lasts. I was changed. I could never walk the tour again but I will always remember it, because I can never forget the day I met evil.

Mel Cross
Pitchcombe, Stroud

Salute: The Ashmolean Museum, Oxford

Everything stops.
Suspended.
The beat of my heart, the squeezing of my lungs;
synapses ceased.
Silence.

Within the anechoic, charcoal-black room,
Only he,
And I,
Exist.

Not a flicker of recognition, but a fireball.
Sinews ignite; lightening; burning.

I had known him for 20 years;
But I never really KNEW him.

Back then he reached somewhere deep inside me;
Deep inside the shadowy chamber where DNA dances,
tangling with passion and soul.
He spoke to me in delicious tongues that he,
And I,
And no-one else I knew,
Spoke.

I took a copy.

I was no longer alone,
Suffocating in the dank-stench of isolation.

We sat in the darkness together;
He showed me the beauty within it.

Life jeered.
People sneered.
Stupid.

'Being an artist is a waste of time', Concurred the cloned.
The mythical gavel of ignorance fell.

I folded up my friend and identity and filed them away
under 'Worthless'.
He was all I kept of ME.
I limped away.

Wandering in the wilderness, the mask of acceptable
normality slid around and buckled on my face.

But here I stand,
20 years later;
Mask-less.

I no longer ignore the screaming of my soul,
And,
unfolding myself,
I put my friend back on the wall.
He sings again.

I am not afraid;
I dance inside.
Resonance.

Everything stopped.
Suspended.
The beat of my heart, the squeezing of my lungs;
synapses ceased.

Silence.
I slid into the anechoic, charcoal-black room,
Where only he,
And I,
Exist.

I hadn't known who he was,
I hadn't known who had painted him,
But there HE was;
IN
THE
FLESH.

'Flesh and Bone.'
Study For Portrait III (After the life mask of William
Blake) 1955.
Francis Bacon.
A name for my taper.

Slicing through the stillness, tears of gratitude salute.
My song roars freely.

And now,
Side by side,
On the wall of my studio,
Hang my tattered photocopied friend and my pristine
postcard from The Ashmolean;
One and the same.

The Full Circle.

I paint until it hurts.
And,
I smile.

Nija Dalal
Manchester

Lost: Manchester Museum, Manchester

She was a teenager when her parents died. My grandmother moved from her one-shared-outhouse-that-was-always-locked-at-night village, to live with her big brother in bigger Mumbai. She flourished, in that sea-bordered city, where waves waft seaweed stink over Chowpatty boardwalk. She's never admitted to flirting, but I imagine the day she asked her brother's best friend, Natverlal, to teach her to ride a bike, there must have been a hint of knowing. He taught her, though she wore a sari, fluttering over her shoulder. And she fell in love with him. She rode a bike and she married for love. In 1930s India, my grandmother did the best a feminist could. With Natverlal and their friends, she talked politics. India and Britain. What Britain took. What India had given. Taking it all back. The freedom, the tea, and smaller things, too. The jewels, in British aristocrat homes, the holy icons and texts in British museums, the sacred animals in British zoos. Perhaps they discussed an Asian elephant named Maharaja, languishing in Manchester's cool winters.She's 90 years old now, living in DC. An oxygen tank by her side, she tells me about those days, when she joined the non-violent movement and found Gandhi the way others find God. With Gandhi's words in their hearts and in their hands, they waited for a new country, with no blood on its streets. For a revolution to win, for the first generation to scream and kick and grow and fight and love under no empire. They raised that generation, my mother's and my father's, in the new born country. And then they sent them away because the revolution won, but it wasn't enough. The new country still has blood on its streets and the screaming and kicking still hurts."This isn't what we fought for," she says. "It was lost."Gandhi, my grandmother told me, wanted India free of its dependence on Manchester, this city, and on Manchester, the cloth named after it. India's dependence, he thought, made India lose itself. This is what I think of while I stare at the skeleton of an Asian elephant named Maharaja, in Manchester Museum. He arrived in Manchester, it says, by walking… from Edinburgh. The fact that he, who was sacred in my homeland, left his warm monsoon home, for the cold hail and drizzle of a grey, stony city, goes unmentioned. He must have felt lost, too.

Linda Delderfield
Swadlincote, Derbyshire

Waste of Space: Birmingham Museum & Art Gallery, Birmingham

On that wall
Surrounded by lights

To gaze in awe
Imagination gone wild

Unique
Indescribable
Diverse and sublime

What was once desirable
What was once is no more
A pitiful greyish tinge of dust outlined

Stripped and bare
White and cold
Disappeared, gone, forgotten, despair

Lonely and neglected hanging space

Cathie Devitt
Erskine, Scotland

Kelvingrove:Kelvingrove Art Gallery and Museum, Glasgow, Scotland

Nestled in the heart of this dear green place,
Majestic it graces the sky-line.

Sir Roger stands tall
beneath a fragile Spitfire,
far from the circus of his youth.
He'll never forget, never retire.

Dali's Christ hangs pitifully on his cross.
Mesmerising many as you'd expect,
whilst Elvis gyrates in gawdy silence,
and visitors express their regret

At missing the Vettriano expo,
Or viewing Kylie's gold lame shorts.
All nationalities, age and creeds,
welcomed to Glasgow, at no entry cost.

Rani Drew
Cambridge

Heritage: Sedgwick Museum, Cambridge

Unlike graveyards where the dead and departed
are buried underground, flattened and unseen
below the inscribed slabs, museums house
the long-gone primordials in grand buildings,
recreate them as they were when alive, limbed
and winged, as if they had never expired.

These still and speechless pre-historic beings,
who were once the breath and beauty of our planet,
yet, like all mortals, vanished into the earth or ocean
without leaving a trace behind, have now emerged
like ghosts out of the dark to tell their tales of
migrations, mutations and exterminations.

Extinct even before humans appeared on the planet,
they are now restored to their original shapes
with exactness – the feat of human technology – inhabit
a man-made paradise, walled and locked with top
security.
Crowds line up to see the ancients perished so long ago.

We gaze at them, mourn their passing away and marvel
at such a heritage of our planet; how once so sterile,
forlorn and lifeless, it became prolific, with breathing
striding giants on land, ocean and air. We gape at
the replicas of these titans from our unknown past.

Now this their urban paradise boasts of our heritage,
where they tell their stories to us who come after them,
and add to the knowledge of our common habitat.
Though divided by unmeasured span of time,
we accept them as our antecedents billions of years ago.

Joss Emmett
Corsham, Wiltshire

Art In Every Form: The Holburne Museum, Bath

Back in time,
down a Georgian street,
up some stone steps,
there's a world at your feet.

Let's go Dutch
with men in ruffs.
Eleven in the navy.
All so tough.

On the other side,
away from the wars,
embroidered gloves
open miniature drawers.

Past The Lobster,
left at the Sam,
family silver
and plates from Japan.

There's a Greek myth
but wearing a crown.
A slice of Guyana
in a Somerset town.

It's getting dark
but don't try to hide.

Don your headphones
and step outside.

Enjoy the ride
and hold on tight.
Magic music.
Living light.

And Xa's just great,
turning tricks from dawn.
A fantastic feeling,
visit The Holburne.

Olive Gallagher
Combe Martin, North Devon

The Cloam Oven: Combe Martin Museum, North Devon

I am the oven made of cloam or clay.
A fire was lit within me to heat my walls each day.
I baked their bread each morning and fish fresh from the sea,
the rabbits snared upon the moor, the scones they had for tea.
I baked potatoes from the garden, their pies and puddings too. Once my walls were heated up I'd cook all day for you. I cooked their stews and Sunday joints, pies, both savoury and sweet – the scent of apples and of blackberries would go wafting up the street. I was such a simple thing. No switch or knob to turn, there were no gas pipes to leak or elements to burn. I could have gone on forever, but the house-wife was so strange, I was replaced one sunny day by a shiny kitchen range! Just light a fire inside me – and I will play my part, I cannot live without a fire. The fire is my heart.

Frances Gapper
Birmingham, West Midlands

The Terror of the Oceans: Natural History Museum, London

The Terror of the Oceans is going to be put in storage, Mr Felix told me. Well I suppose I've got used to it being around, so I felt quite upset. But I told myself, it's probably grown a little stale in the public eye and would benefit from a rest. I continued walking through the galleries. Then I saw a sight that made me feel quite faint – Zillah, our young intern, struggling to lift the Terror of the Oceans from its plinth. I hastened forward. "My dear young lady, that case is far too heavy for you to lift by yourself!"

"No it really isn't, Mr Morgan. I'm strong." Zillah is slim and pale, of boyish appearance, having spent years of postgraduate study under artificial light in universities and libraries. I sprang to her aid, trying to support the back of the case, but our combined efforts proved inadequate and the Terror plummeted floorwards. The display case broke – the Terror lay sprawled on the polished parquet. And there was a very nasty smell.

Mr Felix then loudly appeared, shouting at poor Zillah in quite a brutal fashion, and while attempting to calm him, I uncovered my nose. This was silly of me and the formaldehyde fumes may have caused what happened next to... happen. But what did happen? I remain a little confused on that score. The Terror seemed to rise, to enter me and to speak through my mouth. What it said I really don't know, but soon Mr Felix was backing off and apologising.

Once he was gone, the Terror slithered back into its corpse, leaving me again a weak and mortal man. But Zillah was looking at me with awe. "Mr Morgan, you rock!"

Rosie Garland
Manchester

Sir Thomas Aston at the Deathbed of his Wife: Manchester Museum, Manchester

I reel to a tumult of voices. Laughing
or wailing, I cannot tell.

My collar is too tight, the string of my cuff knotted
into a lump by unquiet fingers.
I am off kilter, as though the artist was a drunkard.

Her hand is paler than my shirt. Face grey as my beard.
Her blood has been given to the bed.

She woke me in a dream last night,
clothed in strange flesh

and said, I am at peace, I pray
you be peaceful too.

Uschi Gatward
London

Toothbrush Ring: Huntingdon War Museum, Huntingdon, Cambridgeshire

It was during a Girl Guide camping trip to St Ives, Cambridgeshire in the summer of 1987. Our group visited Huntingdon Museum. I spent two hours looking round — the first time I'd ever had to be dragged away from something educational.

The exhibit that held me was a ring of dull silver inlaid with a pink plastic jewel. The colours worked beautifully together, and the design was chunky and industrial. It would have sold well now.

The ring was the work of an inmate of a concentration camp during WW2, made from a saucepan and a toothbrush handle.

The toothbrush was clearly the rectangular plastic sort I used myself, in the same sort of colour — toothbrushes hadn't changed much. A two-millimetre slice had been taken from its handle.

The aluminium setting had been hammered into shape, or melted somehow. I must have spent twenty minutes staring at the ring and at the catalogue card, puzzling it out. I wondered how the inmate — I guessed a man — had got hold of the saucepan. Stolen it from the kitchens? When he had hammered it. Late at night? The noise, though. Or over days and weeks, when he was supposed to be doing something else, furtively, far away from the camp guard, ready to drop it in the rubbish at a sign of trouble?

143

Who was the ring for? Was it for another prisoner — a woman, or perhaps a man (I knew about the pink triangles)? Would there be a risk involved in wearing something so attractive in the camp? Especially if you were a man? Why take such risks?

Of course we had learned about concentration camps in school, and we had read some of Anne Frank's diary, and seen clips of television documentaries and dramatisations, so I knew about the camps in a factual sense, but this was the first time I had imagined myself into their reality.

Now my sceptical self wonders whether the story was real or retrospective narrative — even whether the ring was something specifically made to be sold to museums. But it doesn't really matter: it was a way to think about a time and place that I hadn't been able to connect with before. Now I write stories myself and I realise that fiction can be as useful as fact, even when describing the most serious and unimaginable things.

Thomas Giles
Bournemouth, Dorset

Lost Technology: National History Museum, London

"What's that?" Toby asked, pointing at a mess of metal and wires behind the glass.

"I am unsure of its designation, Toby," the soft voice in his head replied. "It does not seem to broadcast on any of the normal channels."

Toby was surprised. "No Wifi?"

"No Wi-Fi, no Bluetooth, no signal of any kind."

Toby stepped forward, pressing his little nose up against the glass case that protected the display inside. "Hmm..." Toby mused. "Could it be a hologram of some sort?"

"Negative," his artificial companion replied. "There are no holo-emitters in range of this display."

It must be real, then, Toby thought. He glanced down at the small plaque in front of the object. "The first random-access memory drive," it said, in tiny letters. "RAM?" Toby said. He'd heard the term in history a few weeks back. The class had gone to the exhibit to see these archaic machines, though such old tech didn't interest Toby. "But why would you make storage you can't talk to?"

"I am not sure, Toby," AI said. "I shall try connecting to it, and monitor for signs of activity. Perhaps it has a faulty data-out mechanism."

"Good idea," Toby said.

"Scanning..." AI said, before growing silent.

Toby started to wander along the wide case, looking at all the machines and parts sitting inside. How do they keep the dust off? he thought.

"Any luck so far, AI?" Toby asked.

He waited a few seconds, but no reply came.

"AI? Are you functional?"

Still no reply.

Toby felt his heart begin to race, thumping in his chest. How would he find his way back to the teacher with no GPS? Who would tell him when he should start back to the school bus? He'd get left behind.

"AI!" Toby pleaded. "Talk to me!" He spun, looking wildly about the room, hoping for someone he recognised. No one's social tags were showing; they were all just strangers to him now. No one was going to step forward. He was lost.

Tears blurring his vision, Toby ran from the room, calling for his teacher and friends.

A small boy ran from the IT History exhibit of the National History Museum. He scuffed past a sign, too tall for him to notice before. It showed the AI icon—a pixelated brain—with it broken in two. Below, it read: "Please turn off your AI before entering this exhibit."

Wendy Goulstone
Rugby, Warwickshire

Earth Mother: Te Papa Museum, Wellington, New Zealand

Take the ferry
from Picton to Wellington
and as you near the shore
you will see the best museum
in the world
Te Papa, the Earth,
built for the people about the people
about Aotearoa
The Land of the Long White Cloud.
Of course, you may love your own museum
in another country
maybe the all-embracing British Museum
or the treasures of Mycenae in Athens
or the Cairo Tutankhamun collection
or a tiny folk museum in your own village
the list is endless
but Te Papa will entrance you
take you on a magical journey
through the heart of this exquisite land
that makes you cry to leave it
and into the hearts of the people
the homes they left
and the new homes they made
their sea-journeys
their struggles
their triumphs
their tragedies

their happy times
two peoples in one land
Maori and Pakeha
two cultures
two ways of thinking
two ways of living
separate but together
no, wait, that isn't quite true
let's be honest
there were difficulties
there were wars
there were mistakes
grave mistakes
there are still resentments
but for an hour or two
let us appreciate individuality
the joys of difference
whilst working together
for the common good
for Te Papa the Earth.
Haere mai. Welcome.

....

NOTES: *Te Papa or Papatuanuku: The Earth Mother in Maori mythology. Aotearoa, or The Land of the Long White Cloud: Maori name for New Zealand. Pakeha: White Europeans. Haere mai: Come here or Welcome.*

Linda Hardy
Alfreton, Derbyshire

At The Museum: Birmingham Museum & Art Gallery, Birmingham

Being brought up in the country, Birmingham shocked me. The noise – day and night no end to it – the shiny new-ness – glass, concrete – people – a swirling vortex of strangers. Despite my well paid job it felt like an exile. The Museum was the only place I felt at home. I loved the calm of well- crafted things, old things, things that weren't for sale but belonged to everyone - treasures not just for rich people, glass cases, not to keep you out but to cherish fragile, beautiful things. Nobody hurried you there. Nobody begged for change. Crocodiles of excited children clutching their clipboards cheered me.

We met on a seat near the The Morte D'Arthur tapestries. The figures, in Burne Jones's world are still, silent. Knights and angels share the same space – an uncluttered world of dark grey trees and dark green grass starred with myriad tiny flowers. We giggled about his name – Galahad. He went in his lunch hour to de-stress. "Do you know that half an hour looking at art lowers your cortisone level – it's proven." In the museum cafe, he confessed he had often noticed me and thought my hair Pre-Raphaelite. "Like Rossetti's Monna Vanna. Luxuriant. Do you know that painting?" Of course. We started to visit churches, in our lunch-time escapes from accounts and retail, at first for the stained glass, later to choose where we'd marry.

On holiday we met John and Rebecca. They were wealthy, stylish, bored. None of us could have guessed how it would end. Burne-Jones, married to Georgiana, had a passionate affair with his Greek model. Georgiana sought solace with William Morris. I remember one afternoon lying on a bed draped in Morris's "Golden Lily" speaking to Gal on the 'phone. "A work conference, yes, tedious. The things one has to do for promotion!" John's fingers caressed my hair. Morte D'Arthur was about Guinevere's betrayal of her husband and king. John laughed, "You take things too seriously. It was fun but it never had a future, did it?" The Morte D'Arthur is all about endings.

The country seems dull, empty after Birmingham. People stare at strangers. I miss Baltis, banter and flat Brummie vowels. There's a Burne-Jones exhibition. I know he'll go. So I will too. Who knows? You should never throw away old things for new. Museums teach you that.

Hilary Hares
Farnham, Surrey

A Gift for the Button Museum: Birmingham Button Museum (now closed)

Small trade sent out by cart
before canals,

the city's wealth
was built on buttons.

Cut from shell or bone
or twisted up from wire

or carved in wood or jet
they tell exquisite stories.

In an unlikely tower block
a shrine is made.

Captured behind glass
each is its own witness,

its name and number
branded on its back.

This, the badge of belief
that sent its wearer to the gallows.

This one so fine
it paid a bankrupt's debt

and this the secret mule
that smuggled gems and drugs.

Clutching a dung-brown bag
against her thin coat

a woman takes the stairs,
flight after flight, on worn-out knees.

I've brought my family, she says
as she reaches a room that floats above cloud,

Twenty one buttons for twenty one lives
cut off in Dachau.

Philip Howard
Preston, Lancashire

Pauline in the Yellow Dress, Sir James Gunn, 1944: Harris Museum and Art Gallery, Preston, Lancashire

It was a risky enterprise, it's true,
To portray a well-dressed, wealthy lady
At the height of wartime austerity,
But that's the kind of thing that artists do
And always will, it's really nothing new;
Still, I'm glad he captured for posterity
That less than enigmatic look we see;
I have no doubt as to its meaning, do you?
That cute presenter on the TV will
Never look at me that way no matter
How much I smirk and simper at the screen
And swear to her divine image that her
Beauty rivals that of a goddess-queen -
Though, if she did - Wow! - that would be a thrill.

Anna Hunter
Belfast, Northern Ireland

A Journey Into Awe: Ulster Museum, Belfast, Northern Ireland

The Ulster Museum is a repository for the childhood memories of many people from Northern Ireland. After two years of refurbishments it reopened in 2009, dazzling us with modern, interactive exhibitions, but just a moment's glance at a familiar artefact brings me back to my first visit as a child and my mental map of the museum as it was in the 1980s and 1990s.

My four-year-old eye was drawn to an intriguing raised glass case in a terracotta coloured room of ancient Egyptian riches. Takabuti, the mummy, imprints herself on your memory – blackened skin, yellow teeth, wavy hair faded to rust and browning linen bandages, offset by her striking turquoise necklace. Though I knew her to be brittle and dead, I wanted to take her one visible shrivelled hand all the same. But any child could resist the notion; if accidentally willed into life she would become the stuff of nightmares.

Expecting a sea life show yet plunged into darkness, all the children wiggled and whispered questions, while parents bid them to wait. The first window revealed a sea floor, illuminated in eerie blue light. Ignoring the narration, we could not help creeping closer to the window to examine the secrets inside. Just as my eyes were adjusting to the dark, a huge yellow eye lit up in the darkness above as the audio track hummed with danger. We all jumped, squeaked, and moved back to the safety of our parents to watch the giant squid with awe.

-In the crystal room, it was as if the riches of the world

were gathered in one place for all to see. As we walked around, the gems twinkled promises of magic. Some had been found on beaches, so the descriptions said – treasure! In a small alcove, darkness and a case of dull stones. As the UV light rose, their phosphorescence revelled in neon disco colours. Fear set in as the Geiger counter started to click... The strangest exhibit is the smell, unique to the Ulster Museum. It's not everywhere, but it lurks there still, waiting to catch my memory unawares from around a quiet corner or down a flight of steps. It transports me back to my four-year-old self, brimming with wonder, giddy with terror, my mind flung open by sights and sounds which will become the markers of happiness.

Sophie-Louise Hyde
Loughborough, Leicestershire

Still Credited to a Woman: Charnwood Museum, Loughborough, Leicestershire

One. This pot was found in a Roman ditch, credited to a woman. Only foundations surviveravages of time –still credited to a woman. Vessels like this often held cremated bone, credited to a woman. A treasure – agedas it rots away, still credited to a woman. Two. Here this ancient church lies silent, dying, credited to a woman. Eighteenth century tombs, a grace forgotten, hidden beneath plasterboard and pew. Also credited to a woman. Grey stones of the grave are solemn. This onecredited to a woman. 'As you lay at rest, may the dovefill your quiet soul with love. 'Also credited to a woman. Three. Corsets stiffened with whaleback bones, credited to a woman. A visible plunging neckline, sheer fabric, of steel rods and midriff torture. Still credited to a woman. Two silk handkerchiefs and some ribbon later, credited to a woman. Compliments of new fashion in 1914 – The all-new 'Backless Brassiere' still credited to a woman.

Lucy Jackson
Leicester

Touching the Past: The Mary Rose Museum, Portsmouth, Hampshire

I had stepped into the Portsmouth Historic Naval Yard under a sky which was heavy and gloomy, the clouds thick and grey, not helping my already depressed mood that day. My family decided a trip to the Mary Rose Museum may just be the perfect remedy to a rain filled holiday thus far.

The outer shell of the building was vast and impressive and even under the dark sky I felt a pang of positivity forming in me. The building housed the Mary Rose, a Tudor ship built in 1510 and which sank in battle in 1545. The ship was discovered in 1971 and raised up in 1982, and the task of resurrecting and conserving this mighty ship began.

This museum doesn't just teach you about the ship and the time it came from, it makes you feel as if you are on it, the decks are reconstructed around the museum and each floor tells a story. Each member of the crew is examined and brought to life and you feel as part of that voyage and battle and that is what makes this museum so special.

Sometimes history can seem so distant, life was so different with so many aspects changed how can you ever identify with it? However sometimes something small but significant and close to our hearts can do that, and that day it was Hatch, the skeleton of the Mary Rose dog. On the website for the Mary Rose it identifies Hatch as one of the most popular exhibitions in the museum and it's because of it being unique but also the feeling that little dog could be any of our pets today. Hatch was the ratter on the Mary

Rose, his bones were found outside the carpenter's cabin and it struck a chord with me that this little dog had been roaming the ship and I could just imagine him sniffing away, getting in people's way but part of the crew and loved.

We change our whole lives but some things always stay constant, people are people and every museum should strive to make you feel something, to have a lasting impact. I came out of that museum having learnt a great deal about the Mary Rose but also a broad smile at the feeling of having touched the past which stays with me even now two years on.

Simon Jackson
Edinburgh, Scotland

Sgriob: The Dufftown Whisky Museum, Speyside, Scotland

On days so cold the woolly hanks
of passers' breath are left when they have gone,
snagged upon the barbs of frozen air,
and auguries of glazed puddles
lend a window
to the mottled bone and shadow
of an impending underworld,
and ghostly sheep led home for long nights
are lost between the mist of field
and their own breath's fog,
on a day such as this the Gaelic shepherds
coined a word unique to their tongue –
sgriob, a term rich in anticipation
describing the itch on the upper lip
before the inaugural sip of the water of life,
that very first whisky of the day.

Tom Jones
Birmingham

The Museum: Newark-on-Trent Museum in about 1953

He was ten years old and spent the holidays with his grandmother. Each day she told him told to go out and do something – not unkindly: he understood that she had other people to bother about and he was quite happy exploring the town. He found mysterious little streets and discovered a ruined castle. He liked the two plaster piglets hanging up on red, white and blue ribbons in the butcher's shop window, but best of all was the local museum, and he kept going back there.

He became familiar with a black and strange smelling wooden machine on which – he learnt from a hand written label - the first books of Lord Byron had been printed (though it failed to tell him who this person was). He could however recognise a picture of a dumpy, grumpy old lady as Queen Victoria. The 'Natural History Room' upstairs was dull, though he was curious about the painted panoramas curving behind the stuffed birds and appreciated that the fake mud at their feet was more convincing than the sheets of glass purporting to be water. The most interesting exhibit however was downstairs: a dozen or so cannon balls formed a dead straight line, not in a glass case but on the floor, starting with a tiny one and going right up to a fearsomely large one which he judged would be far too heavy for him to lift - even if he had dared to do so under the incisive gaze of the silent woman behind the desk.

Much later he read about Lord Byron and recognised

that the printing press had smelt of wood preservative. He also learnt that Newark-on-Trent had been famously be-sieged during the Civil War, hence the cannon balls in its museum. There are no sure answers to the question of why - sixty years afterwards – I should recall them so vividly. It is hardly a matter of historical interpretation: surely Cromwell's soldiers never lined their ammunition up in this way? It was perhaps simply that the way someone had ar-ranged the cannon balls allowed a small boy, wandering again and again round that sad little museum, to see them as a family: lethal weapons had been domesticated and made somehow lovable. As shelves of ornaments in our living rooms demonstrate, we can bestow meanings on inanimate objects simply by the way we arrange them.

I.M. Khalifa
Oxford

Sakura and The Ivory Carver: Ashmolean Museum, Oxford

His eyes fixed, his heart
stilled...
the half carved ivory tree
suddenly coated in a fine ghost
of the Sahara,

Her hands bloomed, her roots
grew...
before the sun closed its eye
and the moon's opened,

desperate not to miss her chance
to stop his honey-yellow lion eyes turning away
from the East.

Too late.

And so the cherry blossoms of
Sakura fell in his wake,
coating his memory so that when the moon
closed its eye and the sun's opened,

the Ivory Carver had not just died
but drowned in
Sakura's
tears.

Chris Kinsey
Newtown, Powys, Wales

The Meteorite Hunters: The Spaceguard Centre, near Knighton, Powys, Wales

I just want to get my hands on the rocks,
and hold drops of lemony desert glass,
to finger the force of flash fusion.

Elemental thrills – I'm eager to divine blast
feeling fragments from Heaven's arsenal –
rare metals metamorphosed by ignition.

The guide's soundtrack grows more sensational –
The next shooting star could take out civilisation.
Return to the Dark Ages. Apocalyptic astronomy.

We savour the threat of extinction, catch breath
for superhero talk of spotting the signs, doing the sums
and saving the planet from sterilisation.

Big guns cue Milton: "Who durst defy th' Omnipotent to arms."
Other plans sound more Tai Chi – cosmic ward-offs
to shift trajectories to glancing fly-bys.

After the tour of the telescope turret we crowd
a small window and orientate ourselves by pointing
at familiar old volcanoes: Brown Clee and tilting
Titterstone.

If we're struck now, here, on the cusp of Stonewall Hill,
the world would sigh with relief - another lucky escape,
another hit in a poorly populated place.

There were eye-witnesses in the Amazon to see
The Sun touch the earth. Skin-witnesses in Siberia in
1908:
The sky split in two. It was so hot I wanted to tear my
shirt.

I couldn't bear it. But then the sky shut tight and
a strong bang sounded. Like a cannon I was thrown
as a hot wind raced between houses.

We'd be newsworthy for a little longer than
the shockwave, set in statistics and You-Tubed
like Chelyabinsk by dashboard cameras.

Brian Francis Kirkham
Salford, Lancashire

Another Earth: Imperial War Museum North, Manchester

Another Earth has landed
down by Manchester's Canal,
Broken in three pieces
By the hammer called War.

You climb the Stair
to reach the pole.
As darkness falls,
on earths remains.

Following a line, commemorating time
that has a start - but has no end
Sounds and smells from the past -
They Greet You.
Shaking you by the hand like an old friend.
The plane at the start,
the tales it would tell
of its old friend Lusitania -
they've salvaged its bell.
It's Just past the smell
of sweet poison gas,
as you take in the wartime things amassed
The T-34 stands just round a bend,
a stones throw away,
from its nuclear friend.
Telling the tales of it winning great battles,
The Cossacks roar out
as the tanks tracks it rattles

And the Trabant car from Germany
stands out and tall
as you read of what happened
on both sides of th' wall.

Uniforms stand in the windows to attention,
as you read of who wore them - it is worth a mention
and you read of the colours, the flags of the men
who are remembered here proudly, never seen of again.

The little red engine
sits in middle, to inspire
telling tales to children,
of men putting out fires

and women delivering messages
by Cycle or by Wire
the tale of those true braves
the one they do aspire

And You wear the old hat
worn by the men
fighting the fires
in fives and in tens,

You land in their place
and think what would you do,
as you read of the stories
from wars one and of two.

Tim Knight
Cambridge

Between The Threshold: Fitzwilliam Museum, Cambridge

White maze for the middle classes,
collect your museum passes at the door,
please
continue through into exhibitions,
photo pictures of art you won't remember the name of
but because you're educated you'll hope to retain its
name, medium, date and frame size of
and equate them with those pieces you Googled before
you came.

Through the double doors
her cries walked down the corridors
whilst cradled in his hands, cradled carefully,
he stood upright in boots on the
newly polished granite, shipped-in, floor.

The art gallery Father and Daughter
are the hidden display
only found in writing in the pamphlet
for today. Some will see them
through cuts in the door,
others may hear them but assume
its ambient art-gallery-played-through-speakers
sound coming from the back room.

Mariia Kukkakorpi
London

Remains: Natural History Museum, London

Remains
are left behind

distantly

past follows even billions of years but never catches, only
drags along, will be investigated, searched and tracked
but never discovered again as it was

but knowledge

that is what
remains

Neil Laurenson
Worcester

Free Admission: Salt Museum, Droitwich Spa, Worcestershire

I was squinting at a skeleton
When the elderly volunteer
Clinging to the till
Twitched into life:

'You'll notice he is well
Preserved
Having endured the crushing weight
Of rock and soil.

I have also endured
A crushing wait,
Decades of toil
And if there's anybody
On or below this earth who deserved

To enjoy eternal sleep
While looking great
It's me.'

Andrew Lemming
Lilbourn, Rugby

Love Among The Exhibits: Various (School Trips: 1975 to 1977)

The Natural History Museum, Tring.
We're going to see every animal that's ever existed. Ever.
Wendy cries because the animals are dead or skeletons.
Miss Birtle hands out a sheet.
We have to find the real names for a giraffe, tortoise and salmon.
Mark calls them "Susan", "Alan" and "Phil".
We've got a picture of a lemur to colour
If we do them properly, we get an Opal Fruit.
I write a note to Dawn
I write: "I like you and want to go out with you."
I ask Wendy to pass it on.
Wendy reads it then tells Dawn I fancy her.
Everyone laughs.
Miss Birtle says I've turned the colour of a proboscis monkey.
I say I don't know what make of monkey that is.
Dawn says she wouldn't go out with me because I look like one.

The Planetarium, London.
We're going to see every planet that's ever existed. Ever.
Wendy cries. She wanted to go to Madame Tussauds.
Miss Birtle hands out a sheet.
We're supposed to find moon names and hidden astronauts.
Mark giggles when he hears the word Uranus.
There's a dot-to-dot picture of two aliens.

If we do them well, we get a Kola Kube.
I write Dawn and my name above the aliens.
I make them hold hands.
I ask Wendy to pass it on.
Wendy shows it to the class and tells Dawn I still fancy
her.
Everyone laughs.
I say it's not true but it is.
Dawn says she wouldn't go out with me because she likes
Mark.

The British Museum, London.
We're going to see all of the History ever.
Wendy cries because the Egyptians are dead or scary.
Miss Birtle hands out a sheet.
We're supposed to find as many animal mummies as we
can
(But not daddies – that's silly).
Mark writes down different words for "poo".
There's a puzzle pyramid. It's the best. It has a maze.
I do the sheet really well and win a Wagon Wheel.
I ask Wendy if she wants to share it.
Wendy smiles and tells Dawn that I'm nice.
Dawn tells everyone that Wendy fancies me.
Everyone laughs.
Wendy blushes and holds my hand.
I say that I like her too and ask her if she wants to go out
with me.

The British Museum is my favourite.

Jane Lovell
Rugby, Warwickshire

Balto the Sled Dog: Cleveland Museum of Natural History, Ohio, USA

It is freezing.
Frost on the road and, on the lawn, a full-size Stegosaurus
delights clambering children;
their laughter bursts out all shazzy with ice.

Inside is warm. An octogenarian in a navy uniform
checks our tickets.

We do the moon rock and the Jeptha Wade gem
collection
then move through Dinosaurs and Fossils.

A cast of Lucy (Australopithecus afarensis) gathers
shadows
from warheads of late Devonian shale fish, hooked and
glaring
in the unforgiving light of glass.

There is so much here...

the profuse:
nine hundred monkey skeletons
and three thousand human,

and the rare:
the only specimen of the small tyrannosaur,
the holotype of the Haplocanthosaurus sauropod,

the most complete mount of a Coelophysis,
replica skeletons of Triceratops and Jane

and, beyond all this, in the Sears Hall,
tucked between an impromptu gathering of Inuit whalers
and wandering caribou, bears built of wire
and horsehair,

Balto the sled dog, sturdy and patient,
in his eyes an Arctic darkness,
the smell of blizzards deep within his fur.

Safoora Masood
Halifax, West Yorkshire

Backbone of the Town: Bankfield Museum, Halifax, West Yorkshire

Inside an imposing Victorian Mansion
A building steeped in history
Has a story to tell
I came here
To acquaint myself
With the building
With the history
That sadly has no relevance
A history belonging to a bygone era
An era that built the town
That attracted the people
That attracted the people to the town
That attracted people from around the world
That attracted my father to leave his home
To work in the factories
In the days when the factories
Were the backbone of the town.

S J Menary
Rugby, Warwickshire

My Ancestor and I: Jewry Wall Museum & the Nasby Battlefield Project, Leicester

I look into the eyes,
Of my ancestor,
Dark, hollow eyes,
That echo through the centuries.

A flash of musket fire,
The stench of gun powder,
And a lead ball,
Lodged in your skull.

Did you know it was coming?
Did you see his face?
The man that killed you,
When you fought for England's freedom.

Did you pray?
Lines of scripture on your lips,
Does your ghost,
Now haunt the battlefields of England?

You would not know me,
Or my gods,
But would you recognise my face?
I see it reflected in yours,

Behind the glass,
I wonder,
Would we have been friends?
My ancestor and I?

Naeem Mirza
Halifax, West Yorkshire

Discovery Road: Eureka! National Children's Museum, Halifax, West Yorkshire

A 20 minute walk
Unaccompanied by an adult
A paid entry
Enabled me to leave
Behind a life I did not fit into
A children's museum
Allowed me
To touch
To be interactive
Hands on in everything that surrounded me
A non-threatening environment
Stimulating in sound, noise and design
A place where childhood was nurtured, respected and
enjoyed
It fed my creativity
It fed my imagination
It would be another year before I could come back
I would have to start saving again
For the entrance fee
To a place meant for children

Zahid Mirza
Halifax, West Yorkshire

Open Spaces: Cartwright Hall, Bradford, West Yorkshire

Out of the rain, out of trouble
Into a place of warmth
Of open spaces
Designed to illuminate
Pictures of the past
To pictures of today
I choose not to follow the crowds
I prefer the quiet, the silence
I glance at the pictures
Hazy eyed
Wishing I had some knowledge
Of who painted what
I like some of what I see
I look baffled by some of it
At aged 8 I have a lot to learn
But for now
I am safe

Frances Nagle
Stockport, Cheshire

With Simon in Florence: The Bargello in Florence, Italy

During our siesta you slept beside me
and I thought again of Alpheus and Arethusa
marbled together in the Bargello.

The blatantly naked river god
has caught the virgin huntress bathing.
Horrified she denies him, and

with not a moment to snatch up her clothes
runs away with the fleetness of a hind
to be caught in the end by exhaustion

and only get away with her precious freedom
when Artemis transforms her into a stream.
This is her story, but the sculptor

to ornament a rich man's fountain,
shows her deliquescent in the god's embrace,
her lips almost touching his.

And then there is her waterfall of hair,
a tease of rivulets tumble down her body,
leave one lovely fulsome breast exposed.

It is her right breast and I foolishly wonder
about the other. If, like mine, it might
have suffered damage. I kiss your shoulder.

Karen Naylor
Cleckheaton, West Yorkshire

Cobra: Wakefield Museum, West Yorkshire

Waiting for the shadows
to lengthen to a threat
I wait in an invisible prison
You see me here, but yet

You do not feel the fear
Nor shiver at my touch
The grey of decomposition
Could never dull my lust

When it came, it was forked
The chains around my neck
Coiled as hollow ribs
Just another to collect

Hold fast to this moment
Before the jaws of truth can bite

Miruna Olaru
London

Am I not a Woman and a Sister?: National Maritime Museum, London

The walk through the museum is fast paced, the curator has a lovely voice and an inspirational face. We stop in the middle of the showroom, where a statue of a kneeling woman is the main attraction. She is set in a black wooden structure, and her eyes are closed, almost like she is praying. Her hands are thrust towards the ceiling and her beautifully carved mouth is half open; below her closed legs, the writing says: "Am I not a Woman and a Sister?"

The curator tells us of the story behind the woman but I cannot take my eyes off her to concentrate. Suddenly, her eyes blink open, and she makes eye contact with me. The burning gaze of the woman makes me flame, and I look at the floor, unsure of what to do.

Am I imagining, or is this real?

Something encourages me to look back and she is mouthing at me, now, so I take a step forward.

No one notices me moving.

She raises from her kneeling position and she becomes bigger, much taller than me. I can see the curves of her body and the movement underneath her clothes.

She gazes at me thoughtfully now, her anger gone, and her eyes are a peaceful blue. "One day, we will all be sisters. Brothers."

I hear her, and I nod, agreeing silently.

"One day we will truly learn from the mistakes of our past. One day, we will be able to walk out in the streets free of fear." She continues and I slowly stop right in front of her, so that I can clearly see her ebony face underneath the harsh, bright light.

"Will it be soon?" I finally croak out, finally managing to find my voice.

"My child, it will take time. Fire and blood will commence until it does. Fire and blood commenced even before. I never rested but it's not enough." She tells me, taking my face in her hands. "Colour, gender, sexuality...is still something that holds us back. Humanity is still discriminating against simple things. It's your generation's turn to fight now."

She then takes a step back and returns to her position, closing her eyes. "Remember these words, now: "Am I not a woman and a sister? One day, we will be free."

Verity Owen
March, Cambridgeshire

'Things': Sedgwick Museum and Zoology Museum, Cambridge

'Things' must be collected,
Lest We Forget,
Things in cases and cabinets,
Things in drawers,
Things in bottles and jars.

Some objects, they say,
tell a story,
Others refuse to speak,
they prefer to remember,
when they weren't in a cage,
and keep their secrets,
to themselves.

Seanagh Palmer – Pilgrim
Maidstone, Kent

The Bayeux: Museum of Reading, Reading

As the tourists gather around,
And stamp about with muffled sound,
I see the flash and hear the click,
Of sneaky pictures, taken quick.
To tell the tale that I'm depicting,
Took long hours of work and stitching,
In Normandy I hang in fame,
But here's my copy, new again.
I hang here, 'neath the steel and glass,
A strong reminder of the past.
Although this version is clean and neat,
I'm still missing things; I'm not complete.
But here or there, it's from me you're meant to learn,
That history and its tragedies will repeat themselves in
turn.

Laura Parkes
Weymouth, Dorset

Grounded by the M-Shed: M-Shed, Bristol Docks, Bristol

Coming home to Bristol,
I find peace and kinship on the dockside.
At the waterfront, the hustle and bustle cafe-culture hides
a bitter history: a city plagued by its dark past.
The s-word is finally coming out from the behind the
shadows.
Bristolians slowly start to talk about our role in slavery.

Lying on the floor in the museum of my past, I am
rooted.
I crawl along a map of my city, with my children and my
mother.
We mark out our own lines, our own family history,
searching for where our grandparents lived, where our
parents grew up.
We find houses, parks, schools that made us who we are,
We find districts and suburbs where we had a first kiss or
a drunken stagger home.
We tell the children about the balloon fiesta and Brunel;
We speak of Christmas Steps and Old Market.
The children run their own tiny hands along the Bath
Road, leaving the river behind.
People crowd around us but leave us alone to follow their
own paths.
Finger upon finger is running along this giant map of a
vast city on this Saturday afternoon.
Each person is looking for their own place on the map, in
this metropolis that is home.

Later we record our own stories in the interactive booths.
How do an get to work and what's the best way to travel?
What do at remember about my years at school?
The M-Shed takes us on a journey back to recent family
history: WW2.
We visit an Anderson shelter and remember Auntie Jean
who lost a leg in a crater in the blitz. She spent 4 years in
Hospital as a young girl.
On the top deck of a 1950s bus, we share stories about
getting around by bus and train, before the smaller
stations all closed.
On the way out we indulge in the city's vibrant future: we
make Chinese paper decorations and attempt some
African drumming!

As I leave the M-shed, I feel an overwhelming sense of
comfort, knowing that this space sums up a childhood
perfectly, as if without saying a word, it knows my past,
my present and my future.
We do not have to shy away from the past, for we are
moving forward in a multi-cultural society.
Bristolians can be a proud people and relish in all that is
good about our wonderful city.

Kauser Parveen
Halifax, West Yorkshire

The Theme of Life: Cartwright Hall, Bradford, West Yorkshire

I came here
In this imposing building
Alone
To shut out the world
To shut out my life
To keep out the rain
I entered into a world
I know nothing about
Except I am surrounded by
The theme of life
Embodied in objects
Of historical, of scientific
Of artistic, of cultural interest
All housed under one roof
All available for me to see
All unavailable for me to touch
All providing me inspiration
Of inner peace
Of inner calm
I know where I can come

Saiqa Parveen
Halifax, West Yorkshire

The Palace Museum: Amar Mahal Palace, India

Enter the Palace
Now a museum
Inside
It houses, exhibits
A golden throne
Paintings, large and small
A library of 25,000 antique books
Its aims, its purpose
To establish a fine arts centre
To collaborate with like-minded institutions of Indian arts
This is more than a museum
Its red bricks overlook the Tawi River Valley
The Palace has sloping roofs, tall towers
A Palace to get lost in
A Palace with only 4 rooms open to the public
All that needs to be seen
Can be seen
I leave wanting more
I leave with my stomach full
I leave with my eyes aglow
A Palace of the past
A museum of today.

David Pearce
Fleetwood, Lancashire

Harriet: Fleetwood Museum, Fleetwood

Harriet's a tough old lady
You can see she's been around
Life for her not always easy
There's been lots of ups and downs.

When she was young she looked so lovely
In a dress of russet brown
Braving out the wind and weather
She was the Queen of Trawlertown.

Under sail she roamed the ocean
Made a friend of flowing tide
Drew the net across the seabed
Found the places fishes hide.

George Fletcher was her skipper – owner
Could have sailed the Spanish Main
Or answered muster on the Victory
When Lord Nelson found his fame.

Harriet became a legend
The toast of any harbour bar
From Mannin's Isle to old Whitehaven
The salty yarns grew near and far.

Fetched up on a beach in Millom
Turned into a playground there
But rescued and brought home to Fleetwood
Long years ago she was born there.

Moored snugly under cover
Harriet's in a museum now
But when they step inside to see her
Hear them gasp, and whisper: Wow!

Author note: 'Harriet' is a Victorian fishing smack, forerunner to the modern day trawler. As one of the last surviving vessels of her type, she is registered on the National Historic Ships Register - Certificate no. 638 and she is also on the National Historic Fleet list.

Mary Pearson
Birmingham, West Midlands

First Nation People: G Catlin - Native American Portraits, Birmingham Museum and Art Gallery, Birmingham

Europeans discovered America?
People were already there!
Faces stare out from the pictures
Dressed Painted Adorned
On show
As outsiders expect.
Blank eyes
They stare remembering
Before the outsiders came
Before they took their lands
And killed their kin.
The bison are gone from the plains
Burial places defiled
Treasures pilfered and bartered
Drink exchanged.
Their souls no longer their own
"But they make a lovely picture".
Do we notice their pain?
Do we recognise their loss?

Lynn Pegler
Northwich, Cheshire

Inspired by a true story. For Tony

Chance Encounter with a Flying Suit: Imperial War Museum North, Manchester

The cotton suit is laundered,
lovingly pressed, precision-folded,
flat, arms tucked behind in a neat symmetrical square,
like a baby sleep-suit on a clean washing stack.

It's a spare, of course, pristine,
as smart as a buffed-up boot,
golden zips glinting in the neon strip, displayed
for all to see in the war museum's wardrobe.

An airline pilot on a casual visit files past,
viewing exhibits with detached interest -
Gulf War Army helmet, Iraqi soldier's parka, "Stop
the Bloody Oil War" poster - when his eye catches the
name

"Kevin Weeks" embroidered gold on black.
Its familiarity slaps him across the face.
The lifeless khaki suit inflates like a corpse
rising from the dead, the bemused, quizzical stare

of his fallen comrade
fires a trance of remembrance:
intense, cool, terrifying Tornado strikes,
endless sand, concrete cities,

his plane on the same mission, only seconds
behind, the scarred wreckage
scorched into Iraqi ground.
Personal friends lost in an impersonal war.

Olivia Phillips
London

Quality Time: Victoria & Albert Museum, London

Light and air sat unnaturally in the room. I supposed it had to. For conservation or something. I looked into a glass case.

'Why's his head so big, Daddy?'

I turned. Rosie had climbed onto a bench behind me. She was kicking her legs energetically beneath it. They ticked back and forth, like her mood, which had oscillated between excited and bored the whole hour we'd been inside the museum.

'Come have a closer look, Rosie.'

She hopped up and we peered into the case. A life-size bust of a man – a king - stared back. Grey, stone, pupil-less eyes bulged from a crown-wearing head. Rosie laid her hands, spread-eagled on the glass and gurned into it. That was all she had for the old monarch. She skipped on to another exhibit.

I took a last look at the stone man. My daughter was pretty astute, I thought. He looked pretty ordinary. Apart from the big head, that was.

Rosie had approached another glass-entombed figure in the centre of the room. She was dancing on the spot before it. The figure was lying on his back, one hand on the hilt of a sword by his side. I read his label.

'Do you know what this is Rosie?'
'Nope.' Her head bobbed from side-to-side, keeping time to some internal tune.

'He's a knight.'

I pointed at his sword for emphasis. Her eyes followed my finger and she looked into the case, wholly absorbed in the way no adult can be.

'Do you know what knights did, Rose?'

She put a hand on her hip. The tip of her tongue crept out onto her lip.

'They went on horses!'

'That's right. Do you know why they went on horses?'

I gave her just a moment.

'They went on horses to fight! Who do you think they fought, Rosie?'

'Baddies!'

I chuckled. I couldn't have put it better myself.

'Why did they put him in the glass box?'

'Well, when he died somebody made a statue of him to celebrate his life. And the museum put him here so that people like you and me could come and learn about him.'

'That's funny. Why didn't they just write a book about him?'
'Well, if they hadn't done this, Rosie, then you and I would have to spend Sundays helping Mummy do Granny's shopping, wouldn't we?'

She giggled and ran onward.

Jenna Plewes
Alvechurch, Worcestershire

Leave Me in the Light: Lynn Museum, King's Lynn, Norfolk

This poem was inspired by seeing Seahenge displayed in Lynn Museum. Seahenge on the Norfolk coast is a prehistoric monument built in the 21st century BC.

When I die
don't put me underground
cut down a giant oak
as they did
four thousand years ago

pull out the stump
drag it across the wide salt marsh
with honeysuckle ropes
upend it where the curlews call

lay me across its outstretched hand
under the sun, the moon
the turning stars

encircle me in
fifty trunks of oak
each split in two
fold a seamless skin of bark around my bier

leave me the smell of fresh cut wood
the shine of pale oak flesh
the sound of wind and tide
birds will clean my bones

midsummer's rising sun will
find me through the keyhole of the east
and when midwinter sunrise looks for me
I will be gone.

Amanda Quinn
Newcastle upon Tyne, Tyne and Wear

Wallace: Sunderland Museum and Winter Gardens, Sunderland

This is the thing. People stare. They point, they touch, they laugh. Often they start writing. Scribble, scribble, scribble. And when I look it's all the same. I mean, come on, use your imagination. I don't miss Africa. I have no yearnings to run free on those hot and dusty plains again. And as for the circus, well, if that was the case I wouldn't have bitten The Great Leonardo, now would I?

No. They're all wrong. I'm happy here as king of this five foot square patch of jungle. Pride of place and most dearly loved. There's the balding patch on my back from the patting but that's an occupational hazard. My cousin at the City Museum lost his tail completely, everyone shaking it 'for luck'. The others I get on with now we're all here together. I no longer eye the zebra or antelope with any interest. My belly is satiated with sawdust.

I'm special. People wish on me. Whisper to me. I'm the only one who knows the caretaker is thinking of leaving his wife. Or that the receptionist dreams of being in musicals.

Keep writing about me. I don't mind. But write the truth.

Joyce Reed
Stockport, Cheshire

Poetry Reading at the Museum: Manchester Museum

We wait in a surreal juxtaposition
of jazz, improvised and echoing
in Victorian space, sitting
under a suspended skeleton
of marine mammal.

Timeless, pastoral tableaux
of glassy-eyed ungulates et al
are posed attractively in death
along the walls.

And the poet speaks
of lives and loves
and other deaths.
Her words swirl and eddy
in the pools of air,
settle on cabinets, like literary dust,
rise to the bleached bones of the whale
in the October night.

Lizzy Ridout
Tynemouth, Tyne and Wear

Hanging Out: National Portrait Gallery, London

Fletcher's the name, Kenneth Fletcher – but it's not by credit of my name that I'm here. It's because of my hat. It's a great hat. I'm wearing it in my portrait. Tam O'Shanter, they call it. I just call it a ticket to the best parties in the world, ever.

I'm a simple man. Peasant you might say, but answer me this – has any other peasant you've ever heard of had his portrait painted, hanging there for all the world to see, with KENNETH FLETCHER printed underneath; like I'm a statesman or a celebrity, and not just some bearded guy with a fantastic hat.

Unlike me, the other guests are all pretty great to look at. A mixed bunch, definitely. Although that's the mark of a good invite list, isn't it?

The parties tend to kick off late. It'd just be too busy otherwise, all those tourists. And their damn rucksacks.

We don't get many turning up from that bunch on the second floor. Stuck up, they are. One portrait by Holbein and you think you're all that. Gheeraerts actually painted Liz I on top of the world, you know? High maintenance- no wonder she never got married. I always liked that Shakespeare bloke though. A bit melodramatic, but he's got a good beard. And an earring always makes a guy look cool. He did turn up once with this bird – Austen, I think it was. She was a good girl. Bit sarcastic, though.

We tend to hang out in groups, but we're happy to mix it up – Gladstone and Disraeli share a room, so they're glad of a break from each other of an evening. Fight like cats and dogs, those two, and it's better to keep things chilled – Oscar Wilde tried to freak things up a bit once, but he's always been into portraits - wrote a book about one, I hear.

I mean, there's always a wet blanket – Virginia Woolf just won't stop knitting – but mostly, they're a laugh. Mike's brother always turns up; he's got a bit of musical talent, apparently. Kate Moss is pretty reliable at a party. The Warhol bunch are great; Joan Collins is a top lass. The Queen never turns up with that lot though – give it time.

Ah, they're always great parties. Shame all the tourists always have to miss them.

T E Samad
Birmingham

Long Live the Bard:Shakespeare's Birthplace, Stratford-upon-Avon

To go, or not to go, that was the question that was presented to me. I instantly knew the answer. The opportunity to visit Shakespeare's Birthplace had arrived on my lap, as if someone from up above looked upon me favourably that day.

I put on my best jacket, my newly-polished shoes and jumped straight into my mother's car, accompanied by my two siblings who didn't share the same excitement or enthusiasm as me. For me, a great day was unfolding; for them, it was just another family day out.

"We're here!" my mother exclaimed as we all stood outside the entrance of the timber-framed museum. Her feeling of happiness equalled mine, perhaps surpassed it. My mother had grown up in Bangladesh reading and learning about Shakespeare, alongside her studies of the Shakespeare of the East, Rabindranath Tagore. She had always wondered about what masterful and soul-moving works of literature could have come into being if destiny had put the two giants together, under the same roof, in front of the same desk.

"I can't believe I'm here," I said to myself as I looked deeply into a portrait of the Bard hung up on one of the walls; its beauty was illuminated by the sunlight pouring in from outside.The replica objects that were carefully placed around the museum didn't fool me, or the other visitors who had travelled great distances from different corners of the world to come here. They probably still couldn't believe that they were actually walking under the same roof that the Bard had slept and dreamt under.

While I was admiring how the aged oak brought an extra sense of rich history, I noticed an old man with teary eyes. I approached him to ask him if he was alright. He had told me that his tears were tears of joy, and that his appreciation for the Bard had always magnified over time. When it was time to go, I said goodbye to him, and shook his hand.

During the drive back, I kept thinking about a comment he made just before we departed from each other. He had told me that Shakespeare is alive, not only in the walls of that museum, but also in every person who hasn't lost the ability to imagine that the world is a grand stage, where life is a glorious play. And amen to that.

Rebecca Audra Smith
Manchester

Sea Dirge: The Manchester Museum, Coral Exhibition

After Watery Ecstatic by Ellen Gallagher

We are washed up,
our bodies brought us children
as surely as weather brings rain.
We give birth beneath the ocean,
sunk as wrecks that dwell
where light does not touch.
Who will come of us now;
volcanoes under water.
Our children
nestle beneath our hearts.
They sing of stories we told them,
violence that strangled and braided
our different songs to one scream.

We are washed up in the ship
of the mouths who made promisesor.
gave us the rope to hang ourselves.
We refused, and now a plank? No, not even
that momentary elevation, that illusion
we will fly before we fall.

We are bundled overboard
like thoughts shut in a coffin
like dreams forgotten underfoot.

Our hands are useless,
grow flippers instead.
Our language denied us,
let us learn a new one.
Atlantis tastes of longing,
here is where we breathe.

Mary Stableford
Oxford

Goodbye-ee: Tate Britain, London, and Ashmolean Museum, Oxford

Grey hotels huddle, all along the prom
A slender pierrot, washed by the autumn dusk, stands
downstage
Pink spotlights fail to warm him. 'Girls' sit round
Cold clenched hands holding down gauze skirts
Against the lusty breeze. Joe fires his jokes
At deck chairs, gaping, sinking in the sand.
Not many in tonight only old folk.
The house will soon 'go dark' like many people's lives.

Guns boom across the waves,
Volunteers are drowning in the mud.
The pianist flexes her fingers, ready to play
A farewell to summer, and a way of life

'Goodbye-ee Goodbye-ee
Wipe a tear, baby dear, from your eye-ee!'

This poem is based on Walter Sickert's painting 'Brighton Pierrots', 1915, of which there are two nearly identical versions, in Tate Britain, London and in the Ashmolean Museum, Oxford

Augustus Stephens
Rugby, Warwickshire

Jina: Victoria & Albert Museum, London

My mouth opens in wonder
As I face you
A stone statue

You sit there
Lotus position
Smiling
Naked
Eyes wide open
Looking at me

I am examined
I am at peace

How can a thing of sandstone
Look into my soul?

You have
Opened my heart

Shanti
Shanti
Shanti

On the way out
I buy the catalogue

Laurence Sullivan
Malvern, Worcestershire

In The Tea Leaves: The V&A Museum, London

She'd done this a thousand times- so many times she actually saw his face in her dreams. Garrick they called him, apparently he knew every major male Shakespearean role by heart- or so the theatregoers said. She had never been one for the theatre, found it too rowdy, crawling with vice. She was the moral sort: temperate, prudent and chaste. There was one little temptation, however, which always grasped her heart whenever she came close to this box. That longing that entangled her, that seemed to whisper in her ear, "Take just a little- they'll never know..."

Tea was worth a fortune- she knew that, everybody knew that. Of course, the caddy itself was worth a thousand fold a pinch of black tea. After all, it was made of pure silver and decorated with the aforementioned actor in his most iconic roles. She could never take the whole thing- that, they would notice. The Lady of the house had entrusted her with the key and that gave her all the power. So, every time her fingers gently caressed the lid of the box and she slid the key into the lock, it made her head spin, her throat grow dry.

Now, her aged fingers grip tightly around the lid of the vessel and open it sickeningly slowly, so that she can savour every second. There it is, a pile of black foliage, which to her shines brighter than any king's gold. She delicately lifts the tea spoon and fills the pot as to her Mistress' wishes, her guests are only minor nobility today- so one spoonful will do. Now for her pinch- no a spoonful- why not a pocket- ful? She buries her hand into the tea and shovels it into her pocket.

Someone's watching. Ginny, the youngest housemaid.

"Now Ginny, you won't go telling no one what you saw, will ya?" The girl stays frozen by the door; her fist clenched tightly and held closely to her mouth- her face an icy mix of shock and fear. "You say anythin' to anyone and I can make life hard for you here..." The statue of ice remains firmly frozen. "Come dear, come here..." The old woman moves to the girl and stretches out her hand to reach for her. Sud- denly, the ice thaws and the girl makes a guttural noise of terror, before briskly turning and running wordlessly out of sight...

Alice Taylor
Cambridge

Cypresses: The Metropolitan Museum of Art, New York City, USA

Just a year before I visited the Met and stood before Van Gogh's work I was at my lowest ebb. Having found out that I had a brain tumour the world seemed darker. What could life hold for me? Medication and scans. No hope of recovery, only attempts to control the tumour and not shrink it. I was already losing fine motor control in my hands. This was not how my life was meant to be. I was only nineteen. Life seemed cruel. Fate was malicious. They care not for who you are, who you love, who you hate, what you have achieved or what you can achieve. An entire life turned upside down by a tiny bundle of cells.

In a welcome reprieve from university work and hospitals I went to the Met and headed up to European Art. Rounding the corner into the space containing Van Gogh's work, my mind was elsewhere. I wandered through the gallery, looking but not really connecting. I was almost at the exit of the space when I stopped in front of Cypresses. The bright blue of the sky drew me in but it was the sheer amount of paint on the canvas that struck me. It was almost too much, giving the piece a 3D effect. These thick, uninhibited strokes made by a man whose life was ridden with anguish yet who was able to express the beauty and vitality of the world around him, even when he, and others, could not see it in himself. He held nothing back. I was fixated. I had never seen Cypresses before and yet it was like a hand reaching out and taking mine, reassuring me that life won't always be easy but it will always be beautiful.

There will always be something worth pouring your heart and soul into, even when you feel like you have nothing left to give. There will always be something worth painting.

As I left the gallery my chest was aching with that sensation that you get when you are intensely happy and sad all at once. Van Gogh's triumph was his art. What shall mine be? Easy. My triumph will be my life and my love of it. I shall grab it by the throat. I shall load my brush and paint with too much paint. After all, what else can I do? What else can anybody do?

Laurence Tilley
Rugby, Warwickshire

Kissing under the Pterodactyl, An Odd Ode: Natural History Museum, London

Marjorie, alas, no longer a girl
after climbing the ladder professional.
Worked twenty years, what for?
To become Senior Curator.
Dusty bones are her great pleasure;
to draw and catalogue each treasure,
and after mortals have wended home
Marjorie toils and works alone.

But! On a day not counted for
in amongst the dinosaurs.
A new Assistant comes along
Keen and willing, handsome Ron.

In museum after dark
they commence to flirt and lark
Oh, the racing, tingling thrill
of kissing under pterodactyl!

Clothing then this pair adjust
by Parasaurolophus -
and hang with unacademic cheek
their undies on Cretaceous beak.

They indulge in rampant sex
afore Tyrannosaurus Rex
notwithstanding gaze so scary
primæval ooze finds last ovary.
Ron Junior though he's still quite young
says he likes dinosaurs, like his mum.

Michelle Tudor
Shrewsbury, Shropshire

Standing Still: Hiroshima Peace Memorial Museum, Hiroshima, Japan.

A boy of no more than eight years old stands on tiptoes peering into a square glass cabinet. Inside lies a watch, remnants of mud still cakes the strap and the face has faded to a dirty-bathroom yellow. Hands unmoving and silent are stuck at 8:15. No time occurred before or after for this piece, it simply stopped at the moment it was savagely torn from the owner's burnt wrist.

A woman walks over the boy and looks down at him, his wide eyes curious. 'This watch belonged to my grandfather,' she said, a mist forming in her eyes. The boy's eyes widened further. 'Is he dead?' he asks innocently. The woman nods and moves closer to the cabinet, she places her hands on the top, reminiscent of a medium placing her hands upon a piece of jewellery, trying to gain some life from it, some knowledge of another time or another life. 'Do you know what happened?' she asks the boy even though she can't see if he is still behind her. 'Yes,' he pipes up and she waits for him to continue, 'Does America really hate Japan?' he asks. She turns to see him looking up at her. She shakes her head, 'No, they don't hate us.'

A man walks over to the two of them, listening in on their short conversation. His face is red and puffy and the woman notices him cut his eyes at her as he grabs at the boy's arm. 'Come on,' he says as the boy tries to squirm out of his grasp, 'How many times do I have to tell you?' The boy stops moving and stands up straight, fear in his innocent eyes, 'Sorry, Father,' he says quietly.

The woman watches them walk away as the boy follows his father in silence, rubbing his arm where his father had grabbed it. He turns back to the woman for a moment and she gives him a warm smile. Another look creeps onto the boy's face and seeing that his father has stormed ahead with several people now blocking his view, he runs back to the woman and hugs her legs tightly, smiling at her and then back at the watch before disappearing back into the crowd towards his father.

Jocelyn Watson
London

Inspirational: National Portrait Gallery, London

Sometimes I wonder where my ideas come from; occasionally there's an answer.

One birthday, when finances were tight, I decided to simply stroll around London where I know there's much to explore that's free. It was her face that awakened my curiosity. She was sitting upright on an armless, backless carved wooden chair, looking dignified and elegant; her long flowing dress, her pointed shoes and her beady necklace draped around her neck, all looking so stylish. It was a black and white photograph taken on 20th June 1930 of an elderly Indian woman I had never heard of before, Cornelia Sorabji. As I read the display attached to the photograph, my curiosity grew. I looked into those serious, focussed eyes and wondered how an Indian woman, born in India in 1866, had managed to become the first woman in history to study law at Oxford University? Her photographic portrait was part of a small display at the National Portrait Gallery. That's when I first saw her. I came across the exhibit as I was aimlessly moving from one section of the Gallery to another. The first woman in history to read law at Oxford; what must it have been like to be the only woman in an examination hall filled with men, many of whom probably resented her very presence? What must it have been like to pass and then not be awarded the degree because you were a woman? She finally got her degree in 1920. When women in Britain were campaigning for the right to vote, Cornelia Sorabji became one of the first women to practise law in India. From Oxford to India, the photographs in the display gave me a fleeting insight into Cornelia Sorabji's life. When I returned home that evening her image reappeared in my dreams. I spoke to my relatives in India, to friends with whom I had studied law, but no one had heard of her. Soon I found myself delving into the British Library archives where I kept asking myself, why our contribution as women, is so often hidden. It was then that I realised that my free birthday foray to the National Portrait Gallery was in fact a gift that was to inspire my first play, Cornelia Calling which, months later, was to receive a rehearsed reading at the Tristan Bates Theatre a few streets away from the National.

USA
Elvis Alves
New York

Three Legged Buddha (after the sculpture by Zhang Huan): Storm King Art Center, New York

Dig a hole
Put your head
in it
Descartes was
wrong
You are more
than a thought

Joann Cook
Arkport, New York

Museum of Glass: Corning Museum of Glass, Corning, New York

You were so unlike the stoic, hallowed halls brimming
with dusty artifacts, or relics of eras gone by.
Not a showy display in shadowed nooks,
of creatures lifeless forms with marble eyes.
My spirit soared on that sunny day
too see your bold, windows rise before me,
glimmering in the morning rays.
Entering your gallery of glass,
bold lights beckon me forth
into a scintillating new frontier
of awe inspiring art...not mere
history, rather the here and now,
the hopes of giving
back, not just taking away.
Shimmering gold spirals
woven with black create a
yellow brick road that I
long to jump on and follow
to worlds unknown. An opaque
rainbow flows upward from
a hidden colour well, both soft
and sharp, full of mystery and intrigue.
Translucent faces that draw my awe
with an enchantment that lures
my smile forth. A myriad of
prisms like fairies dance about
with a sphere of crystal gossamer

their resplendent moon. Precise
pyramids blurred yet lucid
in lustrous hues take me back
in time while catapulting me
forward. Bold lines, graphic
squares, and jagged edges
partnered intertwine shapely
curves with twists and turns.
Playful gnomes in a whimsical
forest of kaleidoscopic
confetti seem to frolic
with a dazzling teapot
quilt whistling a
fanciful tune. Stalks like
golden leaves wave as if
caught on summer's breeze while
the more distinguished pieces
their staid secrets keep from
prying eyes. Floating objects
suspended in a crystal sea,
lead me beyond to a
grid-like hall
of mirrors. I pass by a
crystalline table whose repast
is yet to be seen as I imagine the
glassy curtain billowing softly. A
sky filled with tiffany stars
under which a jazz man played while
dice of chance with hearts on their
string hang in proximity to a
chess game come to life.
In the same way so has my
imagination been awakened,
my soul contented and my
mind awed. As the trial of fire
has refined the glass into
a symbol of undefinable

beauty, I choose
to believe that
the trials of life shall
so refine me.

Torsa Ghosal
Columbus, Ohio

Bata Shoe Museum, Toronto: Bata Shoe Museum, Toronto, Canada

Glass and Copper shoe-box of the Museum
District is giant enough to gobble ancient
pairs of shoes, plus a few shining metallic
legs. In light, the metropolis mounts
its prosthetic limbs and charges. Here,
I collect my steps, forty-two million
feet away from a country called Home: remember

we stumbled on Lord Rama's foot-
steps impressed atop a weeping mountain, four
hours from Bombay? Debated the shoe-size to fit.
I smirked, you twitched, or vice-versa. History

of the paduka—a manual in this shoe-
box— is ready reference. Legends walk
barefoot.

Jessica Goody
Bluffton, South Carolina

"Madonna and Child": Telfair Museum of Art, Savannah, Georgia

Full-lipped Madonnas hold swaddled babies,
their cloths mingling with the dewlaps of dark mantles
and bell sleeves of their Renaissance-maiden gowns.
Sloe-eyed and olive-skinned, their gazes held
by the fat golden cherub in their arms.

The devout look of the mother, sure of the purity and
charm of her innocent child.
Her mantle is brown, the tawny chestnut of a fawn's hide
instead of Massicot bluish-grey, delicate as a dove;
the colour of Mary's mantle, demure and serene.

Red, the most important colour, symbolic of life and
death, joy and evil alike, the longest wavelength in the
human eye;
possessor of infinite names, like the titles of saints.
The red of Christ's blood as he hangs
suspended and sweating in a trance.

She is a Persephone,
sorrow staining aubergine beneath her eyes,
downcast and pensive, her long, elegant fingers
plucking at her face in anguished penance.
Five hundred years later,
her pain still radiates in waves, unrelenting,
her face the chalk-white of bones smeared on canvas.
Vestments rendered in the yellow spices
of Saffron, Gamboge, Burnt Sienna,

Orpiment, Ochre; and in mud of Sienna and Umber,
Medieval browns for monks and priests.
She visits them, aching for solace.

There is a therapeutic quality
in the calm hush of white halls,
the flash of colours alternately tranquil
and joyful emanating from the paint.
Ornate and massive frames
scrolled and curving like waves,
gilt triptychs as thick as mantelpieces
heavy enough to crush a body
should they fall. Five centuries
have not dulled their golden patina,
nor the vivid colours they encase,
Classical colours with antiquated names:

The emerald of Verdigris,
Fabulous as plumage, regal as peacocks,
tinctures distilled to the essence of light, crushed
chemicals toxic and volatile
copper, iron, lead, sulfur, antimony, arsenic.
The magical blue of Azurite,
Ultramarine powder smeared
on the eyelids of dead queens,
the cobalt stain of an unblinking eye
aptly named royal blue.

If she had stood here in this gallery,
gazing into the eyes of stoic, patient mothers
and rosy infants, she might have achieved
a sense of closure from the pain of her lost child.
She did not know that his courage and kindness
would be immortalised by painters.
She knew only love, and suffering.
She did not know that suffering can be
transcended by beauty, and love intensified by pain.

Ojaswee Rajbhandary
Montezuma, New Mexico

The Man in the Khaki Pants: American Museum of Natural History, New York City

I had always been a bratty child, to say the least. While my siblings would spend Saturday evenings gathering grass stains from trips to the park, I could be found with my nose buried in a book. Such "silly" behaviour disgusted me, a prepubescent girl in phase of excessive self-assuredness.

That all changed one unassuming Sunday morning, for that was when I saw the Museum. At first the exhibits were fascinating, but as time passed my crankiness came back in full force. In fact the day would probably have been like any other if it weren't for the man in the khaki pants.

He was a lanky figure, dressed in a shirt covered in tropical flowers and khaki pants; a shock of red hair peeking out from under his safari hat. It was his outfit which made me notice him at first. By the end of his tour it was his enthusiasm that stood out the most. He had been talking about a dinosaur display when I first approached him.

"You look like a zoo keeper," I blurted out. In retrospect I'm surprised he did not even frown in reply. Instead he bent down to eye level with me and said, "well how about I show you a couple of my favourite animals?"

I proceeded to go on a guided tour led by him. Arms waving in the air while his eyes sparkled with the joy, he would practically skip from display to display. It was clear that he cared deeply about the museum and its resident exhibits, and his passion was infectious. I dropped my guard and begin learning, not just studying but actually learning

At last I voiced something that had always bothered me. I asked him why he bothered doing this every day when he could just spend his time learning more. Once more, he bent down and looking me in the eye he said, "what's the point of learning if you are not going to share your knowledge?"

As we were exiting, my mother told the woman at the door about our wonderful tour guide in the khaki pants. Puzzled, she replied while pointing at him. "Him? He's just the janitor."

That day I learned not only that knowledge is useless if you don't impart it to others but that it does not matter where you are in life, you can always teach and inspire.

SJ Wolfe
Worcester, Massachusetts

Padihershef and Me: George Walter Vincent Smith Art Museum, Springfield, Mass

When I was 3 or 4 my Grandfather took me to the Smith Museum in Springfield where I saw my first ancient Egyptian object—it was the outer coffin of a man named Padihershef, although I didn't know this until years later when he and his inner coffin were exhibited at the GWVS museum in the 1980's. This brief encounter would result in a lifelong interest in ancient Egyptian heritage and material culture that has led to my writing a book on Egyptian Mummies— "Mummies in Nineteenth Century America; Ancient Egyptians as Artefacts" (McFarland, 2009) as well as my compiling a database of all Egyptian mummies or parts which have ever come into the United States or Canada. "EMINA" is a work in progress, which currently tracks about 900 mummies through 75 access points. It will be available free, on the web, sometime in 2014. Since I discovered the outer coffin of Padihershef and matching it to the inner coffin and mummy at the Massachusetts General Hospital in Boston, I have spent a great deal of time researching him and his travels in the United States in 1823 and 1824. I have been fortunate enough to work in a rare books library (The American Antiquarian Society in Worcester, Massachusetts) where I have access to hundreds of thousands of pre-1900 newspapers, periodicals, ephemera and monographs. Digitisation of many of these items led to my writing my book as I was not only turning up information about Padihershef but also about hundreds of other Egyptian mummies, including those once owned by the Mormon prophet Joseph Smith. My arduous research also has proved written proof that paper made from mummy wrappings exists and that items printed on such paper still survive. This has in turn led to another project on a bibliography of the paper industry in America through 1900 (a collaborative work with Robert Singerman). The bibliography is 7000 entries long and I am currently indexing it and hope it will be available in 2015. A seemingly chance encounter in a small museum when I was a very small child has led to a lifetime of work and has gained me international regard for my expertise, something I could have never dreamed possible if my husband David Rawson had not encouraged me over dinner to "do something with my mummy stuff."

Acknowledgements

This competition was run in partnership with the British Council.

sampad would like to thank the following people and organisations who have made this possible:

Museums Association UK, Jo Ward, Adult Learners' Campaign, National Council of Science Museums, Engage Conference Birmingham, Birmingham City Council, all India and UK galleries and museums

Everyone who entered the competition.

The Judges:
Chitralekha Basu
Ian Grosvenor
Craig Ashley
Ann Sumner

Sampad receives support from Arts Council England and Birmingham City Council

Competition Judges

CHITRALEKHA BASU likes things that are at least 150 years old. Her first book, *Sketches by Hootum the Owl: a Satirist's View of Colonial Calcutta,* is a critical reimagining of the first work of modern Bengali prose written in 1861/62 by Kaliprasanna Sinha. With hope, her next would have something to do with the life and times of the Indian poet Rabindranath Tagore who also crossed the 150 mark in 1861.

Chitralekha has lived and worked as a journalist in some rather old cities of the world – London, Bangkok, Beijing and her hometown, Calcutta. She has worked for and/or contributed to some of the oldest publications – The Statesman in Calcutta and Times Literary Supplement in London.

Chitralekha is a singer of old Irish and Scottish ballads and Tagore's songs.

Her 11-year-old book club friend calls Chitralekha a museum piece. She's probably not wide off the mark.

IAN GROSVENOR is Professor of Urban Educational History and Director of Teaching and Learning at the School of Education, University of Birmingham, UK and Deputy Pro-Vice Chancellor for Cultural Engagement. He has been involved in antiracist politics and curriculum activity around Birmingham since the early 1980s. Books include *Assimilating Identities. Racism and Education in Post 1945 Britain* (1997and *Children and Youth at Risk* (2009) with Christine Mayer and Ingrid Lohmann. He was a founder member of Black Pasts, Birmingham Futures. He was academic adviser to the HLF supported *Connecting Histories Project* and has worked with the HLF and the National Trust on other projects linked to cultural diversity.. He was Secretary General of the European Educational Research Association 2008-2012; was Academic Adviser to the Heritage Lottery Fund (HLF), and is a Fellow of the Royal Historical Society.

CRAIG ASHLEY is a curator and producer based in the West Midlands. As Visual Arts Producer at mac birmingham since 2009, Craig continues to develop, implement and oversee delivery of the visual arts programme following completion of the arts centre's £15m redevelopment. Collaborating with curators from the region and beyond, Craig has produced a number of exhibitions for mac including: Untitled States (2010), bringing together works by South African artist James Webb in association with producer Anna Douglas; Doug Jones's Alieni Iuris (2011), curated by Indra Khanna and touring nationally; and By the Rivers of Birminam (2012), an important retrospective of the work of renowned photographer Vanley Burke curated by Lynda Morris set to tour internationally. Prior to working with mac, Craig was Curator at Bury St Edmunds Art Gallery in Suffolk and has a keen interest in working with collections and interpretation.

ANN SUMNER joined the Brontë Society staff as the first Executive Director in February 2013. For five-and-a-half years she worked in Birmingham as Director of the Barber Institute of Fine Arts, University of Birmingham, and then at Birmingham Museums Trust. Prior to that she was Head of Fine Art at the National Museum of Wales in Cardiff, and has held curatorial posts at the National Portrait Gallery, the Holburne Museum, Bath, Dulwich Picture Gallery and the Whitworth Art Gallery, Manchester. Ann is a keen Brontë enthusiast and previously worked in Yorkshire in the 1990s when she was Senior Curator at Harewood House. She has published widely and has a particular interest in landscape artists of the late 18th and early 19th century, with her latest publication, 'In Front of Nature: the European Landscapes of Thomas Fearnley' (a Norwegian artist of Yorkshire ancestry who was a rival to Turner in the 1830s, when he lived in England and travelled to Yorkshire) having received excellent reviews.

From the judge's desk

One of my most enduring museum memories is about a two-storied house with peach walls and a calling bell that didn't seem to work. This was in the ancient city of Kannauj that used to be the national capital in the time of the Indian king Harshavardhan (606-647 CE). The Chinese scholar and Buddhist monk Hiuen Tsang (Xuan Zhang) who came here to attend the World Congress of Religions in 637 CE had apparently said it would take any culture at least a hundred and fifty years to build a city like Kannauj.

We stood at the museum door and rattled the iron rings on it for a good fifteen minutes. Just as we were about to turn back a man came cycling by and pulled up beside us, unloading a gas cylinder that was strapped to the carrier. He was the curator of this one-man two-room establishment which had its last visitor more than two months back.

Inside, we were led down impossibly narrow passages. We could only move forward in a single file. There was absolutely no room to turn or step back and admire an exhibit from a different angle. In fact, the gods, spirits, courtesans and kings mounted on pedestals on either side of the ramp had a better chance to size us up, if they so wanted, except that most of them had no heads – bludgeoned centuries ago by vandals eager to leave a mark on what they could not appreciate. Even so it was easy to identify the Sun god, with a little help from Mr Curator who pointed out that the said god always wore a pair of sturdy, sensible shoes.

Museums are often about what we do not see in them. They could be like a code, almost — a cryptograph of signs, images and ideas that may not reveal its meaning to us at the outset. In fact, often a museum piece is quite at odds with what it seems to suggest. Like in one of the entries received for this competition, a sculpture of the three-legged Buddha, by the Chinese artist Zhang Huan, exhibited at Storm King Art Centre, New York, serves as a take-off point for an irreverent little poem challenging Rene Descartes' well-entrenched aphorism about making intellectual activity central to one's life. Sometimes, so the poem argues, the head on your shoulders can save your life by just being there.

Quite a few of the writers who entered this competition wrote about their enduring, evolving, mutating relationship with a museum of their choice. If museums are about that which are dead, ineffectual and in the past, it's only their connection with those who live in the present that give them their meaning. And that link is, as the winning entries in this collection illustrate, often more emotional than cerebral — one more reason to turn the Descartian maxim on its head.

Chitralekha Basu

Bata Shoe Museum, Toronto, Canada

Pringle Brandon Mary Rose Museum, Portsmouth, UK

Pauline in the Yellow Dress, Harris Museum and Art Gallery, Preston, UK

© Harris Museum and Art Gallery, Preston, UK

© Allahabad Museum, India

Allahabad Museum, India

© Calderdale Museums

Bankfield Museum, Halifax, UK

Green and Pleasant Land

Forces of Nature

© Birmingham Museums, UK

Birmingham Museum and Art Gallery, UK.

Chhatrapati Shivaji Maharaj Vastu Sangrahalaya, India

Glass jar, Museum of Broken Relationships, Zagreb, Croatia

The Holburne Museum, Bath, UK

Indian Museum, Kolkata, India

Children viewing Seahenge, Lynn Museum, Norfolk, UK

The Spaceguard Centre, Powys, Wales, UK

© Victoria and Albert Museum

V & A Museum, London, UK

© Victoria Memorial Hall

Victoria Memorial Hall, Kolkata, India

Central Hall, Natural History Museum, London, UK